Improving Reading Comprehension
Grade 5
Table of Contents

3/14

Introduction

We have all watched a child struggle while learning to read. Each new word can be a challenge or a frustration. We have joined in the child's struggle, teaching the skills needed to decode unfamiliar words and make sense of the letters. Then we have experienced joy as the child mastered the words and began to read sentences, gaining confidence with each new success.

Learning to read is one of the most important skills students ever acquire. By the fifth grade, most children are independent, confident readers. The emphasis now can be placed on practicing the valuable skills of reading comprehension. When a child reads without understanding, he or she will quickly become disinterested. Readers need to develop the skill of making sense of new words through context. They need to understand an author's message, whether stated or implied. They need to see how each event in a story affects the rest of the story and its characters. These are all important skills that must be nurtured if a student is to be a successful reader. Reading comprehension is vital throughout the curriculum in school and for success in many other areas of life.

To build the necessary skills for reading comprehension, a reading program should clear away other stresses so that the student can concentrate on the reading. Keeping that in mind, the stories in *Improving Reading Comprehension* have been written to interest and engage the readers. They are short to hold the reader's attention. The exercises are short but effective tools to determine the student's understanding of each story. Given as homework or class work, the two-page assignments can easily be incorporated into existing reading programs for practice and reinforcement of reading comprehension skills.

Organization

The stories in *Improving Reading Comprehension* have been divided into six chapters: School Days; Another Time, Another Place; Facing the Challenge; You Never Know...; Helping Hands; and Mystery and Adventure. The stories are a mix of fantasy, nonfiction, and realistic fiction.

Each story includes one or two comprehension exercises. These exercises concentrate on the student's understanding of the story. Many exercises emphasize vocabulary as well. The exercises include completing sentences, matching words with definitions, writing, finding words with similar meanings, multiple-choice questions, cloze, and crossword puzzles. Each story and its exercise(s) are complete on two sides of one tear-out sheet.

The Curriculum Correlation on Page 4 will allow you to include the reading in other curriculum areas.

There is a Letter to Parents on Page 5, and a Letter to Students is on Page 6. Notifying students and parents of a new activity beforehand will help answer students' questions and keep parents informed.

There are two assessments. Each assessment can be used individually or paired with the other, and given in any order.

Use

Improving Reading Comprehension is designed for independent use by students. Copies of the stories and activities can be given to individual students, pairs of students, or small groups for completion. They can also be used as a center activity.

To begin, determine the implementation that fits your students' needs and your classroom structure. The following plan suggests a format for this implementation.

1. **Explain** the purpose of the activities to your class.

2. **Review** the mechanics of how you want students to work with the exercises. You may wish to introduce the subject of each article. You may decide to tap into students' prior knowledge of the subject for discussion. You might plan a group discussion after the reading.

3. **Remind** students that they are reading for understanding. Tell them to read carefully. Remind them to use a dictionary when necessary if the context is not enough to help them figure out a word.

4. **Determine** how you will monitor the Assessments. Each assessment is designed to be used independently. You may decide to administer the

assessments to the whole class, to small groups who have completed a unit, or to individuals as they work through the book. The assessments can be used as pre- and post-evaluations of the students' progress.

Additional Notes

1. **Parent Communication.** Use the Letter to Parents, and encourage the students to share the Letter to Students with their parents. Decide if you want to keep the activity pages and assessments in portfolios for conferencing, or if you want students to take them home as they are completed.

2. **Bulletin Boards.** Since a key to comprehension is discussion, encourage students to illustrate, add to, or do further research on their favorite stories. Display the students' work on a bulletin board.

3. **Have Fun.** Reading should be fun, and the stories in *Improving Reading Comprehension* will capture students' interest and stimulate their imagination. Fun group discussions, ideas, or games that evolve from the reading will enhance the learning experience.

Improving Reading Comprehension
Grade 5

Curriculum Correlation

Story Title	Social Studies	Language Arts	Science	Math	Physical Education
Shadow Science		X	X		
Lindsey's Odysseys		X			
Marble Magic	X	X			
Late for the Gate		X			
A Kind Rhyme	X	X			
Getting Involved	X	X			
Teachers Teach!		X			
Out of This World		X	X		
Seeing Is Believing	X	X			
Coming to America	X	X			
A New Land	X	X			
The Crystal Palace		X			
Pandora's Box	X	X			
Trouble in Space		X	X		
Woods Wary	X	X			
Ruth Law	X	X	X	X	
Positive Thinking		X		X	X
Against the Odds	X	X			X
I Will If I Want To	X	X	X		
Taking a Stand		X		X	
Jessie Joins the Team	X	X			X
Riddle-ruption		X			
Things Could Be Worse	X	X			X
Two Views	X	X			
Natural Tricks		X	X		
Greener Grass	X	X			
It's an Illusion!		X	X		
Wait and See	X	X			
In the Weeds	X	X			
Helping Habits	X	X			
Lucky Puppy		X			
Taking a Load Off	X	X			
The Three Experts	X	X			
Helping Children	X	X			
The Wand	X	X	X		
Dreamland		X			
Phantom Frights		X	X		
Twin Tricks	X	X			
Clubhouse Mystery	X	X			
Mystery Tree		X			
The Dream		X			
Ocean Adventure	X	X	X		

Dear Parents:

Learning to read is clearly one of the most important things your child will ever do. By the fifth grade, most children are confident, independent readers. They have developed a large vocabulary and have learned ways to understand the meanings of some unfamiliar words through context.

What is equally important for all readers, however, is reading with understanding. If your child reads a story but is unable to describe the events in his or her own words or answer questions about the story, then the reading loses its meaning. Young readers need practice to strengthen their reading comprehension abilities.

With this goal in mind, our class will be working with a book of stories and activities that will reinforce reading comprehension. The short stories are a mix of fiction and nonfiction. The stories are fun, and the one-page exercises are varied. Without feeling the pressure of a long story to remember or many pages of exercises to work, your child will develop a better understanding of the reading and have fun doing it!

Occasionally, your child may bring home an activity. Please consider the following suggestions to help your child work successfully.

- Provide a quiet place to work.
- If your child is reading, help to find the meanings of difficult words through the context of the story. Discuss the story.
- Go over the directions for the exercises together.
- Check the lesson when it is complete. Note areas of improvement as well as concern.

Thank you for being involved with your child's learning. A strong reading foundation will lead to a lifetime of reading enjoyment and success.

Cordially,

Dear Student:

Do you like to read? You can probably remember your favorite book or story. You could probably tell a friend what happened in the story. Maybe you talked to someone in your family about it when you finished reading it.

It is good to think and talk about what you have read. This can help you to remember, to understand your reading, and perhaps to think about it in new ways.

We will be working with a book of short stories. After reading each one, you will be asked to think about the story. Then you will answer some questions. Thinking about these stories will help you become a better, more confident reader.

The stories are a mix of facts and fun. There are stories of school and stories about people helping others. You will read stories of different times and places and mystery and adventure stories. Read carefully and have fun. There is a story here for everyone!

Sincerely,

Assessment 1

Directions

Read the paragraphs. Then follow the directions for each exercise.

One day, one of Peter's classmates had a pool party. He invited everyone from his class. One of the boys in their class, named Joe, usually took the brunt of everyone's jokes because of his size and the way that he dressed. He complained often about everything. Peter wasn't sure whether he complained a lot because kids picked on him, or if the kids picked on him because he complained a lot.

At the party, Peter's friends began to pick on Joe almost immediately. They made remarks about his bathing suit and his goggles. They picked on the way he walked. They kept most of this to themselves, however, until someone got the idea to push him into the pool. They all thought Peter should do it because no one could get mad at Peter. Peter felt pressured by his new friends to push Joe into the water. "He probably can't even swim," thought Peter. Then another thought came to him. He realized that the boys had challenged him. He also realized that he had another challenge before him. He was unwilling to pick on Joe. Maybe if he said so, and refused to take part in their mischievous plan, then the other boys would stop, too. On the other hand, they might decide that Peter was too chummy with Joe and start treating Peter the same way!

Choose the word that best fits each sentence. Write the word in the blank.

1. Joe usually took the _____ of everyone's jokes.
   bunt   brunt   meaning

2. Peter felt _____ by his new friends.
   pressured   impressed   pressed

3. Peter knew the boys had _____ him.
   changed   fooled   challenged

4. Peter was _____ to pick on Joe.
   unable   unwilling   afraid

5. He refused to take part in their _____ plan.
   mischievous   missing   helpful

Go on to next page.

Directions

Answer each question about the story. Circle the letter in front of the correct answer.

6. Why did Peter's friends pick on Joe?
   a. because he was mean to them
   b. because he was different from them
   c. because they were told to
   d. because Joe could not swim

7. Why did the friends want Peter to push Joe into the pool?
   a. because they could not do it
   b. because Peter could not swim
   c. because no one could get angry with Peter
   d. because Joe had pushed Peter into the pool

8. Which is the right decision for Peter to make at the end of the story?
   a. to join his friends and push Joe into the pool
   b. to leave the party and not deal with the problem
   c. to push Joe into the pool and jump in with him
   d. to tell his friends that he will not push Joe into the pool

Rewrite each sentence. Use a word with the same meaning from the Word List in place of the underlined words.

Word List
complained   remarks   realized

9. The boys made <u>comments</u> about Joe's bathing suit and goggles.

_____

10. Peter <u>had the thought</u> that the boys had challenged him.

_____

11. Joe <u>found fault with things</u> often.

_____

Write which challenge you believe Peter should take and why. Write four to five complete sentences on a separate sheet of paper.

Assessment 2

Directions

Read the paragraphs. Then follow the directions for each exercise.

The benefits of helping another person in need are more than first meet the eye. Of course, we all know it's the nice thing to do. Think about yourself in a situation where you might need help. Then imagine how you would feel if someone helped you. At the same time, helping other people helps you in ways you may not have considered. When you reach out to other people, you always feel better about yourself. It gives your life more meaning and brings you out of your own small world.

You may think of a way to surprise someone with unexpected help. Planning to help someone can give you something to look forward to. Helping other people is a great way to make friends, too. Even a seemingly small thing, like helping someone to pick up dropped books or groceries, will bring a smile of appreciation from the recipient. The next time you see that person, you can bet he or she will remember your courtesy, and it will bring another smile—to both of you.

Read each sentence. Choose a word from the story that has the same meaning as the word or words in bold print. Write the word on the line.

1. The **rewards** of helping other people can be many. _____

2. Think of yourself in a **position** where you might need help. _____

3. Even **what may seem to be** small things that you do can be very helpful to others.

   _____

4. People will show their **thankfulness** with a smile._____

5. They will remember your **kindness**. _____

Go on to next page.

Name_____   Date_____

Directions

Think about the story you read. Then fill in the blanks of the following paragraph with words from the story.

Helping others can bring you **6)** _____ that you may not have

considered. If you think of yourself in a similar **7)** _____, you will know

how it would feel to have some help. Helping not only makes the **8)** _____

of your help feel better, it will make you feel good, too. Planning a surprise of

9) _____ help can give you something to look forward to. People

may show their **10)** _____ in many ways, but the good feeling you

get from helping others will be all the reward you need.

Write *true* or *false* next to each sentence about the story.

11. _____ Helping others can help you, too.

12. _____ You should expect a gift in return for helping someone.

13. _____ People only need help with large problems.

14. _____ Helping others is a good way to make friends.

15. _____ Most people will forget about your courtesy.

Write about a way that you have helped someone. Tell how it made you and the person you helped feel. Do you think your help was appreciated? Use four to five complete sentences.

_____

_____

_____

_____

_____

Shadow Science

Harry liked playing ball on the school team, and he liked his classes—all but science. The teacher and the book were always talking about things like cells and molecules and about how things worked.

Harry couldn't get interested in thinking about the insides of things. He loved trees, but he wanted to look at them and enjoy them whole. He didn't care much about why they grew.

Harry loved storms, sunshine, and wind. He loved to feel the wind as he and his dog, Shadow, ran into it. He liked to lie beside Shadow in the sun. He even liked holding Shadow as they looked out at a storm. But Harry didn't care about how weather was made. "I couldn't make the kind I want anyway," he said.

Then one day Shadow got very sick. Harry and his parents took the dog to the veterinarian hospital and had to leave him there to be treated. Harry began stopping at the vet's every night after school to see how Shadow was doing. The man explained very carefully why Shadow was sick. He told Harry how Shadow was being treated and how the new medicine had been developed by scientists.

Long after Shadow was home and well, Harry was still learning about what made animals healthy and sick. He had become very interested in science, and he was studying hard to become a veterinarian.

Go on to next page.

Directions

Answer each question about the story. Circle the letter in front of the correct answer.

1. The one thing Harry does not like about school is _____.
   a. having to play ball
   b. his science class
   c. looking out at storms
   d. having Shadow following him there

2. At first, Harry just wants to _____.
   a. know what causes weather
   b. find out how plants grow
   c. talk about molecules
   d. see and feel nature

3. To Harry, Shadow is _____.
   a. someone to share things with
   b. just an animal in the way
   c. an animal that he could study
   d. really his parents' pet

4. Harry changes his mind about science after _____.
   a. he begins to study about science harder
   b. a new medicine saves Shadow's life
   c. he and Shadow watch a storm
   d. a veterinarian comes to Harry's school

5. The veterinarian explains to Harry that _____.
   a. he couldn't change the weather no matter how much he knew about it
   b. Shadow will never get well
   c. scientists develop new medicines to help sick people and animals
   d. veterinarians make lots of money

Lindsey's Odysseys

When Lindsey first walked into our class, she had a strong effect on people. She didn't seem like anyone else. It wasn't just that she dressed and acted differently; it also seemed strange that she didn't seem to care about those things. She didn't look, for example, like Marcia Gainer, who never wore a pair of socks that didn't match the color outfit she was wearing. She didn't talk like Elise Penrod, whose sentences all sounded like ones heard on television commercials. There was something else about Lindsey, though. When she walked, her chin was always level. When she spoke to you, her eyes always gazed directly into yours. She seemed to be very sure of everything and to know things that none of the rest of us fifth-graders knew.

The first time Lindsey came to my house on a Saturday afternoon, I asked her (as any polite hostess would) what she wanted to do. "Today is a good day for an odyssey," she said. I thought I must have misunderstood her.

"Excuse me?" I questioned.

"An odyssey! You know, we'll set off for a wandering-about, and we'll have great adventures on the way. I'll be Lindseus, Prince of Thorun, and you'll be Ariel, my lifelong friend and companion. We'll travel to Prendor to rescue the Princess Berea."

"Is this some computer game or what? I've never heard of this one."

"No. Don't you remember meeting Theseus and Ariadne last week? We will follow their course if we're able."

Then I remembered reading in class about mythological heroes. But wasn't this carrying it a little too far? I started to wonder about Lindsey. I couldn't wonder long, though, because before I knew it, she was running out the door and calling me to follow. I still had my doubts, but off I went.

I soon learned that time spent with Lindsey was filled with stories of mythical beasts and heroes. We built a palace in the woods and from there, we sailed on many important journeys. It was some of the most interesting time I spent that year.

Go on to next page.

Name_____   Date_____

Directions ──────────────────────────────

Think about the passage you read. Then fill in the blanks of the following paragraph with words from the Word List.

Word List

misunderstood   hostess   doubts   odyssey
lifelong   mythical   companion   mythological

Lindsey was different from other fifth-graders. I wanted to be a good

1) _____, so I asked her what she would like to do. She suggested

it was a good day for an 2) _____. I thought I must have

3) _____ her. She said she would be a prince, and I could be her

4) _____ friend, or 5) _____.

I remembered reading about the 6) _____ heroes that

she spoke of in class. I had my 7) _____ about Lindsey's

odyssey, but I went along. Lindsey and I spent many hours imagining

adventures with 8) _____ beasts and heroes. It was a

very interesting time.

Use the Word List above to choose the correct word for each meaning. Write your choice on the line.

9. for the length of our life _____

10. did not understand _____

11. one who spends time with another _____

12. uncertain thoughts _____

13. relating to myths _____

14. a person who entertains guests _____

15. from mythology _____

16. a long journey _____

Marble Magic

Bonita's cousin Kirby showed her the marble he found in the ground while helping Aunt Helen in the garden. It was large and clear, except that inside there were pearly white swirls, some faint blue streaks, and a spot of gold that caught the sun and shone like a star. "I roll it in my left hand and make a wish," Kirby said, showing Bonita how to do it.

"And will your wish come true?" Bonita said.

"Almost always," Kirby said, smiling and holding the marble up to look at the sky through it.

"Do you have another marble?" Bonita asked. "How I'd love to have one! I'd roll it in my hand and wish that Miss Logan, my teacher, thought I was the best student she ever had."

"You can have this one," Kirby said. Bonita took it very carefully and thanked him with a smile.

"Did the wish you just made come true?" she asked.

"Yes," Kirby said. "I wished that there was something important I could give you as a gift."

At school, Bonita watched closely to see any signs that Miss Logan had been affected by her wish. Bonita began working harder on her homework and listening very carefully to any instructions the teacher gave. Soon Bonita noticed that Miss Logan was smiling at her and giving her more attention. "It's true," Bonita thought. "The marble really works!"

Go on to next page.

Directions

Answer each question about the story. Circle the letter in front of the correct answer.

1. The "star" inside the marble is made by _____.
   a. faint blue streaks
   b. pearly white swirls
   c. a spot of gold
   d. the sky showing through it

2. Bonita wants to wish that _____.
   a. Kirby will think highly of her
   b. Miss Logan will think highly of her
   c. the star in the marble is real
   d. the marble has red inside it

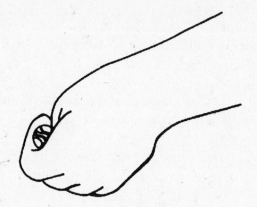

3. Kirby gets his wish when _____.
   a. Bonita asks for the marble
   b. Bonita works harder at school
   c. he finds the marble in the garden
   d. Aunt Helen gives him the marble

4. A good word to describe Kirby is _____.
   a. selfish
   b. foolish
   c. serious
   d. generous

5. Bonita probably got her wish because _____.
   a. Kirby rolled the marble in his hand
   b. Aunt Helen talked to Miss Logan
   c. she worked harder at school
   d. she forgot about the marble

Late for the Gate

"We won't get there before the plane leaves if you don't hurry," shouted Derek's mother. "You'll find a message that says they couldn't wait for you."

Derek jammed the last things into his suitcase, picked up his ticket, and took the stairs two at a time. He was breathless when he jumped into the car.

Derek's class had carried groceries at the local store every weekend to earn money for a special class trip to Washington, D.C. Derek had arranged for the work with his father, who was manager of the store. Now Derek and his mother were racing through heavy traffic to get to the airport. Derek was yelling for her to drive faster.

"It's too dangerous, and I'd lose my license if a police officer noticed us," his mother replied. "I'll drive straight to the airline door. You just leave your bags with the agent and meet your class at the gate."

When they arrived at the entrance, Derek's mother pointed out the official waiting at the door, said a quick good-bye, and sighed as Derek rushed into the airport.

Two days later, Derek's parents received a short note from Derek's teacher: "The class's hotel has been changed. Address is now 2607 15th St. All students are keeping diaries. I think you will find them interesting reading!"

Go on to next page.

Directions

Answer each question about the story. Circle the letter in front of the correct answer.

1. Derek is going to Washington, D.C., with _____.
   a. his mother
   b. his class
   c. his parents
   d. his father

2. What is the meaning of *agent* in this story?
   a. the cause of something
   b. a very old person
   c. someone who represents the company
   d. an airline pilot

3. Derek's mother sighed because _____.
   a. she was tired
   b. she did not like to drive
   c. Derek forgot his ticket
   d. she was relieved that Derek made it

Write *true* or *false* next to each sentence.

4. _____ Derek's class worked to earn the money for the trip.

5. _____ Derek's class was flying to Pennsylvania.

6. _____ Derek's mother took her time getting to the airport.

7. _____ A police officer gave Derek's mother a ticket.

8. _____ All the students kept a diary of their trip.

A Kind Rhyme

Everyone was to write a limerick and get up and read it to the whole class. Brenda was really good at rhyming, so she finished and read several limericks while her classmates kept working on theirs. Brenda's first limerick went like this:

There once was a young girl named Nell,
Who couldn't subtract very well.
    She took six from ten,
    Looked puzzled, and then,
Said, "I've the answer right here, but won't tell."

Billy looked over at Nell, who stared down at her desk when everyone laughed. Then he looked at Brenda at the front of the room and made an awful face. Before Billy could think of a riddle, Brenda jumped up and read another riddle that went like this:

There's a young boy in our class named Billy,
Who can make his face look quite silly.
    It's been scrunched up that way
    So much, it may stay.
You'd think he'd learn not to, but will he?

Billy got an idea. Soon he got up to read this:

There once was a young girl named Nell,
Who had a funny limerick to tell.
    Her classmates were glad
    It made nobody sad,
And the teacher told Nell she did well.

Go on to next page.

Directions

Answer each question about the story. Circle the letter in front of the correct answer.

1. Brenda's first limerick makes fun of Nell because Nell _____.
   a. is not there
   b. is looking down at her desk
   c. can make rhymes more quickly than Brenda
   d. finds arithmetic difficult

2. Billy doesn't like Brenda's first limerick because _____.
   a. it doesn't rhyme
   b. it hurt Nell's feelings
   c. it is all about him
   d. it doesn't make sense to anyone

3. Billy makes a face at Brenda because _____.
   a. she is being unkind to Nell
   b. he wants her to laugh
   c. he likes her first limerick
   d. she has stolen his idea

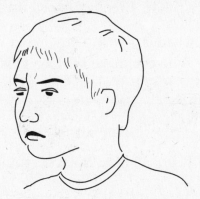

4. Brenda's second limerick is her way of _____.
   a. telling Billy that she likes him
   b. keeping the class laughing
   c. telling Nell she is sorry
   d. getting back at Billy

5. Billy's limerick tries to tell Brenda that _____.
   a. people don't like being insulted
   b. Nell is actually good at arithmetic
   c. limericks are not supposed to be funny
   d. her limericks are the best

Getting Involved

Robert and Andrew were working on a project in social studies. They had been studying the revolutionary war in class. Their project was to find the names of any "freedom fighters" who played a role in the founding of America.

At first, Robert and Andrew thought it sounded like a dull thing to do. Then they discovered that the people on whom they were doing the research were really interesting. They agreed that what they had done was quite exciting.

"How come nothing like this happens anymore?" asked Andrew. "It just doesn't seem like it's anything that we have any connection with—like it's anything that affects us."

"You're right," answered Robert. "Some of the people we've read about were not very old, but they were really involved in the struggle for rights and for freedom. What about our freedom?" Robert was really dramatizing now, trying to speak the way he imagined Patrick Henry spoke.

"Why do we study history, anyway?" said Andrew. "Isn't it partly so we can learn to participate and be good citizens...or something like that?"

"I know what we should do," offered Robert. "Let's ask Mr. Newman if we can discuss some issues that do affect our lives right now. We can make it a project to become involved. We could write an article for the school newspaper, or even write to the governor...or our senators!"

"We can call the President of the United States!" shouted Andrew.

The boys knew they were getting silly now, but after they returned to class, they suggested the project to Mr. Newman, and the class began talking that day about issues that might be important to them.

Go on to next page.

Name_____ Date_____

Directions

Read each clue. Choose a word from the Word List to find an answer to fit each clue. Write the words in the puzzle.

Word List

governor   issues   connection   participate

involved   senators   dramatizing   revolutionary

ACROSS:

4. relating to a complete change
6. link
8. things being discussed

DOWN:

1. to join with others
2. in the U.S., the head of a state
3. to act in a dramatic way
5. members of the senate
7. mixed up in

Name _____   Date _____

Teachers Teach!

If you ask most teachers what the best part of their job is, they will probably say "teaching." That may sound strange at first, because that's what teachers do. However, teachers have to do much more each day besides teach. Teachers must plan and prepare for the lessons. They have paperwork to do for administration. They have hall, recess, and lunch duties. Many teachers volunteer for extra activities. They coach, guide the yearbook staff, or run science and math fairs. Teachers can get so busy that the time they spend working with their students becomes precious!

Teachers go to college and take exams to become qualified. During their teaching careers, teachers must keep up-to-date on new teaching techniques. To keep their teaching skills sharp, they continue to take courses. They do all this so that they can teach young people the wonders of science, the importance of literature and art, and the lessons of history. They try to find ways to make learning fun. Teachers want to make a connection with their students. When teaching is at its best, even the teacher can learn—from the students!

Teaching is a profession that allows one person to directly influence another. Teachers can watch their students learn and grow with the information and the learning tools the teacher has supplied. In this way, teaching can be an extremely rewarding job. It can also be very frustrating when students can't, or don't want to, learn. Good teachers are special people who can take the stress and frustrations of teaching and balance them with the rewards. We should never underestimate the value of our teachers!

Go on to next page.

Directions

Answer each question about the story. Circle the letter in front of the correct answer.

1. The main idea of this story is _____.
   a. that anyone can teach
   b. that teachers have to go to school, too
   c. that there are too many things for teachers to do
   d. that teachers are dedicated to teaching

2. Once a teacher goes to college and passes the exams, _____.
   a. there in nothing left to learn
   b. the teacher must continue to take courses
   c. the teacher must take a coaching position
   d. the teacher will probably find a different job

3. What are *techniques*?
   a. students
   b. lessons
   c. methods
   d. courses

4. According to the story, what can frustrate a teacher?
   a. taking courses after college
   b. running a science or math fair
   c. learning new things from students
   d. students who don't want to learn

5. If the frustrations become greater than the rewards, a teacher might _____.
   a. stop teaching and choose a new career
   b. ask for a new group of students
   c. tell administration to stop sending paperwork
   d. ask one of the students to take over

Out of This World

"Humpf!" grumped Mr. Nedles from the sofa during the nightly TV newsblast. "What a waste of galaxy dollars it is to build that station out in space!"

"It's not a station, Dad," Halmar said. "It's a whole space city! It's the first space city ever! I hope to survive in one after I have all my cells."

"Actually," Halmar's mother said, "it's more like a town. It's supposed to hold only 1,000 individuals."

"That's right," Mr. Nedles grumbled across long arms folded on his chest vest. "You'd get bored fast in such a place—no room for star-glow sledding, air surfing, or meteorball in that place. You have the craziest and spaciest ideas!"

"Well," Halmar said, "there will be 3-D television with a different show on each wall. There'll be all kinds of good things to eat on cable menu."

"And you can walk to the end of your world in only fifteen midi-timers," Mr. Nedles snorted.

"Actually, Mansack," Mother began, "it doesn't sound so bad. You might like it yourself. You never get off that sofa once you get home from work."

"Besides," Halmar said, "I will be able to rocket over to other space cities whenever I like. I can come back here to Mars and visit you once in a while. With the right kind of space suit, I could even go see what life is like on the planet Earth."

Go on to next page.

Directions

Answer each question about the story. Circle the letter in front of the correct answer.

1. The news that Halmar and his parents are talking about is that _____.
   a. Mars has just won a meteorball tourney
   b. Earthlings have invaded Mars
   c. Halmar must leave the planet Earth
   d. the first space city is to be built

2. Mansack thinks that Halmar will get bored with _____.
   a. a place with no room for sports
   b. traveling to different planets
   c. collecting galaxy dollars
   d. star-glow sledding

3. Mother suggests that Father is _____.
   a. eager to go into space
   b. a bit lazy at home
   c. dreaming of going air surfing
   d. a secret agent from Mars

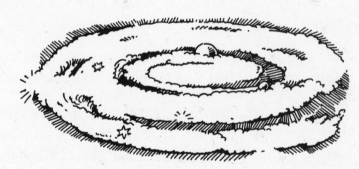

4. This story takes place _____.
   a. on Earth
   b. in a space city
   c. on Mars
   d. in a space bus

5. Halmar could be said to be _____.
   a. adventurous
   b. contented
   c. lazy
   d. frightened

Seeing Is Believing

When Columbus plotted to sail the blue
In fourteen hundred and ninety-two,
He had no screw loose under his hat—
He knew that the world was round, not flat.

"Our eyes deceive," he said to the queen.
"The world is round, and I mean
to prove it to all. I'll sail to the edge
and then a bit farther, but I'll fall off no ledge!"

"Seeing is believing," the good queen suggested,
And believe she did, when his theory was tested.
Do we see what we believe or believe what we see?
Is the question for Columbus, the good queen, and me.

Go on to next page.

Directions

Rewrite each sentence. Use a word with the same meaning from the Word List in place of the underlined words.

Word List
deceive   plotted   theory   ledge

1. Columbus <u>made a plan</u> to sail across the ocean.

_____

2. Columbus told the queen that our eyes <u>do not show us what is really there</u>.

_____

3. He was not worried about falling off a <u>shelf of rock</u>.

_____

4. When Columbus sailed, he tested his <u>idea with no real proof</u>.

_____

The poem asks, "Do we see what we believe or believe what we see?"
Write four or five sentences describing the difference between the two.

_____

_____

_____

_____

_____

_____

Coming to America

Elise held tight to her mother's hand at the railing of the huge ship. They had a nice room on the ship, but Elise had been too excited about moving to the United States to sleep. Her father, who was from New York, had come home right after World War II; and now she and her mother were coming to live with him.

Elise was thinking about what her grandmother, who was very French, had told her before she left France. "Elise, you are very lucky," she had said. "You are a citizen of both France and the United States, two wonderful countries. But someday you must choose to be a citizen of one or the other."

Then Grandma told about Elise's great-grandmother, who came to New York on the way to Canada in 1910. She did not have her own room—only a cot deep down in a ship with many other persons. Elise decided that her ancestor must have been even more frightened than she was now.

Elise saw the beautiful lady with the torch getting closer and closer. Grandma had told her to watch for the Statue of Liberty, France's gift to America in 1885. Her great-grandmother must have seen it, too, when she arrived.

"You are lucky . . . but someday you must choose." The words rang in her head. Elise missed Grandma and France already, but, oh, she was excited to be coming here!

Go on to next page.

Directions

Answer each question about the story. Circle the letter in front of the correct answer.

1. Elise's father is a citizen of _____.
   a. France
   b. Canada
   c. the United States
   d. both France and Canada

2. Elise's great-grandmother moved from _____.
   a. France to Canada
   b. America to France
   c. France to the United States
   d. Canada to the United States

3. Compared to Elise's voyage to America, her great-grandmother's trip was _____.
   a. less exciting
   b. not as frightening
   c. much shorter
   d. not as comfortable

4. As she arrives in New York, Elise feels _____.
   a. as if she has made a big mistake
   b. both frightened and excited
   c. completely alone
   d. very, very seasick

5. Someday Elise will have to choose whether she will _____.
   a. be a citizen of the United States or a citizen of France
   b. live with her parents in New York or her great-grandmother in Canada
   c. stay with her mother or go back to her father
   d. be a citizen of two countries or just one

A New Land

Dear Elizabeth,

I can't begin to tell you what I have experienced since leaving home. It was so sad to leave all of you and everything I have known, but this experience has taken my breath away. It has not all been easy by any means. There have been severe difficulties. There have been times when the dangers were mounting, and death seemed around the corner. To have survived seems like quite an accomplishment now.

Life is quite different here. Everything is different—what we eat, how we eat, our choice of things to do. There are many more opportunities for work and interesting ways to occupy our time. Not everyone would find them as enjoyable as I do. I have been keeping a diary to document all that happens here and to be able to remember how unlike home it was—and yet how similar in many ways. I hope that you will be able to come some day. There are no words to describe this experience. Everyone must make it his or her own.

Yours sincerely,

Edward

Go on to next page.

Name_____ Date_____

Directions

Read each sentence. Choose a word from the Word List that has the same meaning as the word or words in bold print. Write the word on the line.

Word List

enjoyable   document   accomplishment
diary   occupy   severe

1. Edward writes that there were **extreme** difficulties on the journey.

_____

2. He felt that it was an **important thing achieved** when they survived.

_____

3. In the new place, there are many interesting ways in which to **use** one's time.

_____

4. Edward finds many of the new ways **pleasant**.

_____

5. Edward is keeping a **record of daily events**.

_____

6. He wants to **record** all that happens for the future.

_____

Write *true* or *false* next to each sentence.

7. _____ Edward has experienced much since leaving home.

8. _____ He finds it easy to describe his experiences.

9. _____ The trip was a difficult one.

10. _____ There is not much to do at the new place.

11. _____ Edward will have no way to remember his experiences.

12. _____ The new place has nothing in common with the place he left.

The Crystal Palace

The castle of the Great King rose above the snowy plains like an iceberg. When they saw it for the first time, many travelers thought it to be a mirage. Yet it was real to touch, a palace made of crystal as pure as the ice of a mountain stream.

The castle was built by soldiers captured by the Great King in battle. It was said that you could hear the cries of those soldiers in the fierce arctic winds that whipped around the castle walls.

Within the castle stood the high throne of the Great King. Many a traveler had trembled in the cold before this great golden seat of government. Yet the Great King did harm to no travelers and was always eager to hear news from any faraway land.

Go on to next page.

Name _____   Date _____

Directions

Answer each question about the story. Circle the letter in front of the correct answer.

1. The Great King's castle is made of _____.
   a. ice
   b. iron
   c. crystal
   d. gold

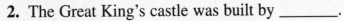

2. The Great King's castle was built by _____.
   a. soldiers
   b. winds
   c. travelers
   d. icebergs

3. The noises heard around the castle walls are made by _____.
   a. soldiers
   b. arctic winds
   c. travelers
   d. the Great King

4. The high throne must have been made of _____.
   a. wood
   b. crystal
   c. ice
   d. gold

5. A good word to describe the castle is _____.
   a. cold
   b. jolly
   c. dark
   d. crowded

Pandora's Box

Many years ago, the people of Greece made up stories to explain the events in their lives that they did not understand. Because they did not have scientific explanations, they told myths in which gods and goddesses ruled Earth and skies. One of those myths explained why there is unhappiness on Earth.

The god Zeus was angry with the humans for accepting the gift of fire. He felt that only the gods should have fire. So he thought of a punishment for humans. He made a woman and named her Pandora. She was given the gifts of intelligence, grace, beauty, and kindness. Zeus gave her two more gifts before he sent her to Earth. The first of these was curiosity; the second gift was a sealed box. Zeus told her she must never open the box.

For a while, Pandora lived happily on Earth. Nevertheless, every day she passed by the box many times, and it began to intrigue her. She wondered what could be inside. Her curiosity grew with each day. Finally, she could stand to wait no longer. She decided to take just a peek inside the box. She struggled to get it open, and when she did, all kinds of horrors flew from it and into the world. Illness, envy, anguish, and many other evils circled Pandora's head and flew out her door to plague humankind for eternity. When Pandora finally got the lid back on the box, only hope remained inside. In this way, Zeus had his revenge, but humans would always have hope.

Go on to next page.

Name _____   Date _____

Directions

Read each clue. Choose a word from the Word List that fits each clue.
Write the words in the puzzle.

Word List
plague   envy   anguish   punishment
intrigue   revenge   eternity   humankind

ACROSS:
5. the human race
6. the desire to have what is someone else's
7. a price to be paid for wrongdoing
8. time without end

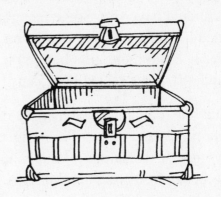

DOWN:
1. great pain and suffering of body or mind
2. to continue to annoy with disease and misery
3. an act of harm in return for an earlier act
4. to arouse curiosity

Improving Reading Comprehension 5, SV 5803-5

Trouble in Space

The astronaut stood twenty yards back from the opening of the cave. She had been in the cave for forty hours now, and there was still no change in her view. The glare from the murderous sun still streamed into the cave opening, threatening death to anyone who walked out into it.

The astronaut looked at her timepiece. "Forty-eight hours ago..." she thought, "two Earth-days ago, everything was fine." She sat down again on the black cave rocks and thought about the accident. She thought about the blinking warning lights and the blasting sound of the siren. She remembered the captain's calm as he steered the small spacecraft toward this place, the nearest planet on which to land. They had had a rough landing on the dark side of the planet, away from the heat of the sun. The sun's heat could destroy any living thing on this desert world.

After landing, the astronauts had dragged the spacecraft into a cave. There they could work to repair it without worrying about the return of the sun. The captain had sent her to explore this neighboring cave, in case they should have to remain here for Earth-days. She had gone deep into the cave but had found no water, no moisture, and no plant life. When she came back up, she found her path blocked by the 200-degree heat of the sun.

Go on to next page.

Directions

Answer each question about the story. Circle the letter in front of the correct answer.

1. Why doesn't the astronaut have her spacecraft?
   a. Another astronaut had borrowed it.
   b. It was destroyed when she landed.
   c. It is being repaired on another planet.
   d. It is being repaired in another cave.

2. Why is she on this planet?
   a. She is on vacation.
   b. She is looking for another astronaut.
   c. This planet was the closest after her spacecraft broke down.
   d. This planet is the best place to have a spacecraft repaired.

3. How does she feel about being on the planet?
   a. She thinks it is a good place to have her spacecraft repaired.
   b. She would like to be able to explore the planet.
   c. She does not care where she is.
   d. She is afraid that they will all die.

4. Why must she wait until the sun goes down?
   a. The spacecraft will not be repaired until then.
   b. The other astronauts will not be ready to leave.
   c. The sunlight would destroy anyone who moved too close to it.
   d. They will need to see the stars to steer.

5. Why is the astronaut alone?
   a. She lost the others during the crash.
   b. The captain sent her to explore the cave.
   c. The others left her behind.
   d. She wanted to rest.

Woods Wary

Jason didn't know why he had agreed to come along. He had always been afraid of things that he did not know, and now he was about to face hundreds, maybe thousands, of "unknowns." His cousins, Kerri and Allan, were unpacking the camping gear as Jason looked around. He said to himself, "This is the wilderness, all right."

Jason's uncle was setting up the tent just behind them. Jason felt guilty that he was the only one not doing anything. "Hey! What can I do?" he asked, trying to sound enthusiastic.

"Firewood," Kerri answered immediately. "Somebody has to go gather the firewood."

"Right, the firewood," Jason replied. "Where do they keep it?"

Kerri looked at him strangely. "We're in the woods, Jason. The firewood is all over the place. Just make sure it's clean and dry. Okay?"

"Right," he assured her. "I'll get the clean, dry stuff." He walked toward an overgrown trail behind the car. "Here we go," he thought. "You wanted to find out what it was like to camp out in the woods. You're about to find out."

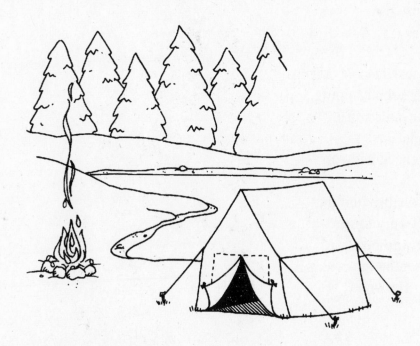

Name _____   Date _____

Directions

Answer each question about the story. Circle the letter in front of the correct answer.

1. Jason doesn't know why he agreed to go because _____.
   a. he does not like camping
   b. he is tired of camping
   c. he does not like his uncle
   d. he is afraid of things he does not know

2. Jason feels guilty about not helping, so he _____.
   a. hides from his cousins
   b. asks how he can help
   c. tries to look busy
   d. helps set up the tent

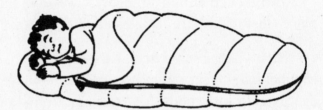

3. What is the meaning of *enthusiastic*?
   a. like a joke
   b. afraid
   c. very interested
   d. calm

4. You can tell that Jason's cousins _____.
   a. have never been camping
   b. have never built a fire
   c. have not met Jason
   d. are experienced campers

5. Jason will probably find that _____.
   a. camping is only for girls
   b. he was right to be afraid
   c. camping can be fun
   d. there is no firewood

Ruth Law

Throughout history, there have been many women who have become accomplished pilots. Women, however, were not encouraged in their pursuit of a pilot's license. It was not considered proper or even possible for a woman to fly a large plane! In spite of this, these women did become pilots and did fly planes. Several of them even broke aviation records.

One of these women was Ruth Law. In 1916, Ruth attempted to fly from Chicago to New York City in one day. She would set a record for uninterrupted flight across the country. Ruth encountered some difficulties as she prepared for her flight. She had tried to get a larger plane, but was denied by the manufacturer. He did not believe a woman could handle a larger plane. The small plane had to be outfitted with a second gas tank, but to compensate for the extra weight of the gasoline, the lights were removed.

It was November when Ruth attempted her flight. Her plane did not protect her from the weather in any way. She dressed in many layers of clothing and put a skirt on over the top, as women were expected to wear skirts always in those days. She had to navigate with maps that were attached to her leg, and a compass.

Ruth was forced to land before she got to New York because she ran out of fuel. She landed safely, refueled, and started out again. It began to get dark, however, and without her lights, Ruth could not fly at night. She had to land two hours short of New York City. She had not made her goal, but she had set a record for nonstop flight—590 miles! She flew into New York City to great fanfare the next day.

Go on to next page.

Directions

Read each clue. Choose a word from the Word List that best fits each clue. Write the words in the puzzle.

Word List
accomplished   pursuit   aviation   navigate
uninterrupted   fanfare   compensate   encountered

ACROSS:

5. to direct the course of a ship or aircraft
6. skilled from practice
7. without stopping

DOWN:

1. celebration
2. having to do with aircraft
3. met
4. to make up for something
8. attempt to get something

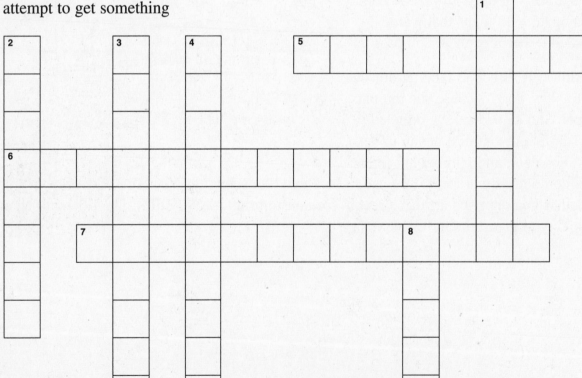

Positive Thinking

"This is the worst day of my life!" Jenny thought. She had just dropped the ball one of the Redbirds hit into center field. Two of their runners crossed home plate, and Jenny's team was behind 3-0. She saw her parents smiling encouragement in the bleachers.

The Redbirds had got their first run when Annie Nolbe hit a home run. The ball came down just outside the fence and Jenny made a grab for it but missed.

Then Jenny struck out at bat—twice in three innings! Now she had caught and then dropped the ball. It was an error, and the Stingers were losing 3-0. "I'll just quit playing baseball," she thought. "That's the least I can do."

In the last half of the last inning, the score was still 3-0. There was a Stinger on each of the three bases. It was Jenny's turn to bat. She knew that she could win the game for the Stingers by hitting a home run. That would bring the three players on the bases across home plate. Then Jenny would cross it, and the Stingers would win 4-3. She looked over and saw her mother and father on the edge of their seats. "I can do it. I can do it!" she kept saying.

Whack! Jenny's father rushed down and lifted her to his shoulders as she crossed home plate. "A grand-slam homer!" he kept yelling, bouncing her around.

"It was the least I could do," Jenny mumbled.

Go on to next page.

Name _____ Date _____

Directions

Answer each question about the story. Circle the letter in front of the correct answer.

1. Jenny thinks it is the worst day of her life because she _____.
   a. has to hit a home run
   b. hurts herself on the fence
   c. strikes out and makes an error
   d. has to go sit on the bleachers

2. The name of Jenny's team is _____.
   a. the Redbirds
   b. the Nolbes
   c. the Stingers
   d. the Homers

3. Before the final inning, Jenny thinks she should _____.
   a. quit playing baseball
   b. go sit with her parents
   c. make one more error
   d. congratulate Annie Nolbe

4. The final score of the game is _____.
   a. 4-4
   b. 3-0
   c. 3-1
   d. 4-3

5. Jenny feels that hitting a home run _____.
   a. is an impossible thing to do
   b. helps make up for her mistakes
   c. embarrasses her father
   d. makes her a hero

www.svschoolsupply.com

© Steck-Vaughn Company

Unit III: Facing the Challenge

Improving Reading Comprehension 5, SV 5803-5

Against the Odds

It is May 1989. The Red Sox are facing the Angels in a major-league baseball game. On the mound stands a rookie pitcher named Jim Abbott. He is facing the veteran Red Sox pitcher Roger Clemens. The Red Sox are favored to win. However, as the game progresses, it becomes clear that their batters are no match for the young man on the mound. The Angels win the game. Jim Abbott is a major-league success!

This was just one more in a lifelong series of successes for the talented and hardworking Jim Abbott. His story, from Little League, to the Olympics, to the major leagues, is an inspiring one. It is even more so because Jim was born with only one hand. Neither Jim nor his parents had ever considered his handicap a reason for special treatment. Jim always had dreams. His parents never discouraged him from pursuing any of them. Their encouragement, along with his own hard work and perseverance, allowed him to go straight to the top as a baseball pitcher.

Jim's message to young people is one of setting goals and working toward them. He is also an example to all who know him of what it means to be a team player. It seems that Jim is a special person not because he was born with one hand. He is special because he is a shining example of goodwill and achievement in spite of it.

Go on to next page.

Directions

Rewrite each sentence. Use a word with the same meaning from the Word List in place of the underlined words.

Word List
pursuing   perseverance   goodwill   achievement

1. Jim's hard work and <u>continuing to try</u> helped him to succeed.

_____

2. Jim's parents never stopped him from <u>going after</u> his dreams.

_____

3. Jim's major-league win was a great <u>thing that he did</u>.

_____

4. Jim's <u>friendly attitude</u> has helped him to be a good team player.

_____

Choose the word that best fits each sentence. Write the word in the blank.

5. Jim was called a _____ because he was new to major-league baseball.
   veteran   rookie   ranger

6. Roger Clemens was a _____ ballplayer.
   rookie   vacant   veteran

7. Jim did not let his _____ interfere with his dreams.
   handwriting   happiness   handicap

8. His story is _____ to everyone.
   persuading   inspiring   inferior

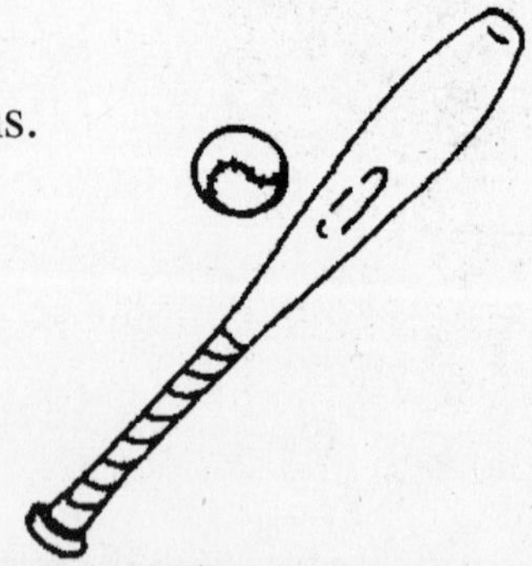

I Will If I Want To

I'd like to dig a trench just once,
but "No! you can't!" they'll say.
They'll say I shouldn't grease a car,
but I'm going to someday.

I can play baseball just as well
as my big brother, Bill;
I bet I can make a big-league team,
and if I want to, then I will.

And as for Bill, if he decides
to run his house someday
because his wife would rather work,
then they should have their way.

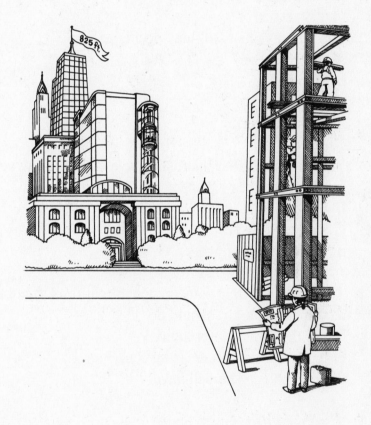

When I look up and see those men
building way up high,
I think I'd like construction,
building things up to the sky.

If I want to be a doctor,
I'll study till I'm blue.
I'll be one—or a lawyer,
if that's what I would do.

But if I decide to design clothes
or be a perfume clerk,
don't tell me, "That's the thing to do
because it's women's work."

I'm a person, just like Bill.
I dream, and so does he.
We want to choose from everything
and be what we can be.

Go on to next page.

Directions

Answer each question about the poem. Circle the letter in front of the correct answer.

1. The girl is afraid people might tell her not to grease a car because _____.
   a. it is men's work
   b. she can't drive one yet
   c. she has a brother who wants to do it
   d. she plans to be a doctor

2. The girl says that Bill may decide to be a _____.
   a. trench digger
   b. homemaker
   c. lawyer
   d. perfume clerk

3. The girl thinks that in order to be a doctor or lawyer, she will first need to _____.
   a. design clothes
   b. turn blue
   c. study a lot
   d. do construction work

4. The girl thinks that some people might think that being a perfume clerk is _____.
   a. something a girl should do
   b. not the right job for a girl
   c. harder work than greasing cars
   d. not a choice she will have

5. What the girl wants to do is _____.
   a. become a clothes designer
   b. build tall buildings
   c. be a housewife
   d. choose what she wants to be

Taking a Stand

Peter was relatively new to his school, but he had made friends very quickly. He had become something of a celebrity because he was from California. All the kids here thought that California was one big movie scene with actors walking around everywhere. Peter didn't really want all the attention, but he guessed it could be worse. He saw how some of the unpopular kids were treated. Sometimes, when he was with a group of his new friends, it was difficult not to get caught up in some of their games. That was all right when they were just having fun and not hurting anyone, but when they began to taunt and embarrass other students, it made Peter uncomfortable.

One day, one of Peter's classmates had a pool party. He invited everyone from his class. One of the boys in their class, named Joe, usually took the brunt of everyone's jokes because of his size and the way he dressed. He complained often about everything. Peter wasn't sure whether he complained a lot because kids picked on him, or if the kids picked on him because he complained a lot. At the party, Peter's friends began to pick on Joe almost immediately. They made remarks about his bathing suit and his goggles. They picked on the way he walked. They kept most of this to themselves, however, until someone got the idea to push Joe into the pool. They all thought Peter should do it because no one could get mad at Peter. Peter felt pressured by his new friends to push Joe into the water. "He probably can't even swim," thought Peter. Then another thought came to him. He realized that the boys had challenged him. He also realized that he had another challenge before him. He was unwilling to pick on Joe. Maybe if he said so, and refused to take part in their mischievous plan, then the other boys would stop, too. On the other hand, they might decide that Peter was too chummy with Joe and start treating Peter the same way!

Peter decided to take the risk. He told his friends that he thought it was a dumb idea, and that he wanted no part of it. He said he thought it was mean, and that they could all have more fun if they would just leave Joe alone. Surprisingly, the boys did not put up a fight. They grumbled a little, but mostly they agreed with Peter. The party turned out to be fun for everyone, and no one bothered Joe for the remainder of the day.

Go on to next page.

Name _____   Date _____

Directions

Think about the passage you read. Then fill in the blanks of the following paragraph with words from the Word List.

Word List

brunt   celebrity   mischievous   unwilling
taunt   pressured   unpopular   surprisingly

Peter was treated like a **1)** _____ at his new school because he was

from California. But his friends sometimes **2)** _____ him to join them in

their **3)** _____ pranks on **4)** _____ students. Peter

was **5)** _____ to embarrass and **6)** _____ these

students. There was one student in his class who took the **7)** _____ of

many jokes. When Peter decided to take a stand and not push Joe into the pool, he found

that his friends **8)** _____ went along with him.

Write *fact* or *opinion* in front of each sentence about the story.

9. _____ Peter has just moved from California.

10. _____ Peter has found it easy to make friends.

11. _____ Peter's friends are mean.

12. _____ It is unfair to tease people.

13. _____ Peter's friends respect Peter's opinion.

www.svschoolsupply.com

© Steck-Vaughn Company

Unit III: Facing the Challenge

Improving Reading Comprehension 5, SV 5803-5

Jessie Joins the Team

This was the worst year of Jessie's whole life. Her parents were insisting that she had to play a spring sport. They said she needed more physical activity to go along with her reading. Jessie loved to read! She could spend almost every afternoon lost in her books. What was wrong with that? Obviously, her parents had a problem with it because they were making her do something else! Now she had to choose between basketball and softball, and she hated sports. She didn't know how to play those games, and all the girls would be making fun of her the whole time. They had probably played for several seasons now so that they all knew what they were doing.

Finally, Jessie choose softball. Her father took her to get a new glove and bat and a bag to keep her things in. She liked the way the glove felt on her hand—its soft, leathery texture and smell. But she didn't even want to get out of bed the day the practices started. She realized, however, that she had no choice. Her parents were not going to let her back out of this, so she thought she had better make the best of it. She put on a brave face and joined the other girls on the field after school.

The first thing Jessie found out was that not all of the girls had played softball before. The second thing was that she wasn't a bad hitter once she figured out the proper stance and swing. Her coaches were very patient, and they kept working with her until she could hit most of the pitches. She needed a lot more practice, but she knew she would only get better. She began to look forward to improving her game and then playing a real game with another team. She hated to admit it, but after only one day of practice, she was determined to become a good player and help her team to win some games!

Go on to next page.

Directions

Answer each question about the story. Circle the letter in front of the correct answer.

1. Why is Jessie upset at the beginning of the story?
   a. Her parents are making her go to summer camp.
   b. Her parents are making her read all the time.
   c. Her parents are making her choose a sport to play.
   d. Her parents are telling her what sport to play.

2. What does Jessie like about the things her father buys?
   a. the feel and smell of the glove
   b. the weight of the bat in her hand
   c. the bag that holds all her equipment
   d. nothing

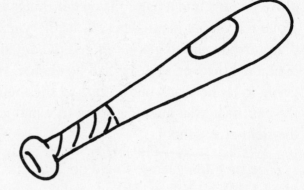

3. Why does Jessie go to the field for practice?
   a. She wants to go.
   b. She knows she has no choice.
   c. She knows the girls who are there.
   d. She has no other place to go.

4. What does Jessie find out at her first practice?
   a. All the other girls know how to play.
   b. Her coaches did not know she was coming.
   c. She can be a good hitter.
   d. Softball is as bad as she thought it would be.

5. Which one of these might be a lesson from this story?
   a. Don't judge a person until you walk in his or her shoes.
   b. The squeaky wheel gets the grease.
   c. Don't judge a book by its cover.
   d. Don't knock it until you have tried it.

Riddle-ruption

Wanda was having a good time just sitting and reading when Sue and Billy came in.

"I have a riddle for you to guess," Sue said.

Wanda looked up and replied, "Excuse me, but I'm reading now. This is the best part of the book."

Sue went right on. "What has lots of ears but doesn't hear a word you say?" Wanda looked at her with a smile, thinking, "That sounds like you two."

Before she could speak, however, Billy began jumping up and down yelling. "I know! I know!" Then he jumped too close to Wanda and bumped his nose on the soft chair.

Wanda put a marker in the book and closed it. She said, "Corn. Now, you tell me. What knows and knows till it bumps its nose?"

Sue and Billy thought about it but could not think of an answer. Then Billy said, "All right. When do you go to see but not to look?"

"When you're at the ocean," Wanda replied. "Now please, let me finish my book."

Go on to next page.

Directions

Answer each question about the story. Circle the letter in front of the correct answer.

1. As far as Wanda is concerned, Sue and Billy are _____.
   a. entertaining
   b. unwelcome
   c. challenging
   d. too smart

2. The answer to Sue's riddle about something that has lots of ears but cannot hear is _____.
   a. a chair
   b. Billy and Wanda
   c. corn
   d. the ocean

3. Wanda thinks that the best answer to Sue's riddle is _____.
   a. corn
   b. Sue and Billy
   c. the ocean
   d. Wanda

4. The answer to Wanda's riddle about something that knows and knows is _____.
   a. the ocean
   b. the bookmark
   c. Sue and Billy
   d. Billy

5. The answer to Billy's riddle about when you go to see but not to look is _____.
   a. at night
   b. when you are reading
   c. when you are at the ocean
   d. when you close your eyes

Things Could Be Worse

"My family is going to Aspen for the holidays! Do you believe it?" Karen fairly shrieked into the phone. "My dad just told us. Six days of great skiing and getting a great tan. Who could ask for a better present?"

Karen's family arrived at Aspen in the middle of the day, so they didn't have much time on the slopes. The next morning, however, they were out right after breakfast. Karen went directly to the more difficult slopes. She soon regretted this because, by midafternoon, she had already fallen three times. Once she came so close to the T-bar that they had to stop it. It was all so embarrassing and disheartening. She headed for the lodge.

After getting something hot to drink, Karen slumped down in a seat across from a girl who looked about her age. "You don't look like things are going too great today," the girl commented in an offhand way.

"To say the least," Karen responded with little interest in offering details.

"Well, you know what they say..."

"No, what do they say?" Karen interrupted with a snap.

"Oh, they say things like, 'It could be worse,' 'Things will get better...'"

"Try, try again..." Karen added with something of a snicker.

"Yeah, you know what I'm talking about."

"Somehow those things just never seem to make me feel better when things are going wrong."

"They sure don't! But you know, there is some truth to all of them. Did you ever hear the one, 'I cried because I had no shoes, and then I met a man who had no feet'?" the girl asked with a smile so broad that Karen had to think there was something more behind her question. "I used to think that was pretty dumb, until it became true."

Karen felt lost in the discussion, until the two of them got up to go and ski together, and she saw that her friend only had one leg. The girl, whose name was Alicia, and she spent many hours together in the following days, and Karen learned a great deal about courage and true spirit. Afterwards, they corresponded for many years and shared many of their deepest feelings about life.

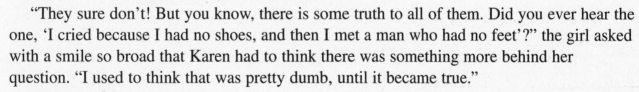

Go on to next page.

Directions

Choose the word that best fits each sentence. Write the word in the blank.

1. Karen _____ going to the difficult slopes.
   relieved   regretted   disliked

2. By _____, she had fallen three times.
   morning   evening   midafternoon

3. Karen found her difficulties _____.
   disheartening   humorous   painful

4. The girl said something to Karen in an _____ way.
   awful   sarcastic   offhand

5. Karen and Alicia had a long _____.
   disgusting   discussion   dinner

6. Afterward, the girls _____ for many years.
   corresponded   collapsed   skied

Write *true* or *false* next to each sentence.

7. _____ Karen's family was on the mountain to go hiking.

8. _____ There was not much time to ski the first day.

9. _____ Karen almost skied into the T-bar.

10. _____ Karen met Alicia in the lodge.

11. _____ Alicia was born with only one leg.

12. _____ Karen thought Alicia was courageous.

Two Views

Two brothers, Mack and Ian, went wilderness camping with their father. They carried a tent, life preservers, and some food in a silver canoe. They went into the lakes and woods of northern Minnesota. Each boy kept a journal and wrote in it each day. Here is what Mack wrote for April 3:

What a day! My shoulders ache from paddling. Ian fell out of the canoe. He got confused and swam away from us. I was afraid we would never see him again. On shore this evening, it got dark too fast to put up the tent. Bears got into the food, so we had to keep a big fire going all night. That, the bears, and the weird cry of the loony loons kept me awake all night. We ate fish again, and I am so hungry for a hamburger that I could eat one raw.

Here's what Ian wrote in his journal about that day:

What a day! It began with a refreshing morning swim when I fell out of the canoe. I knew that I would tip Dad and Mack into the lake too if I tried to climb back in, so I swam to shore while they paddled beside me in case I needed help. Tonight, we ate a delicious big bass Mack caught. Later, we had some furry visitors, and that was very exciting. Then we settled into our sleeping bags beside an open fire, and I went to sleep listening to the wonderful song of the loons.

Go on to next page.

Name_____   Date_____

Directions

Answer each question about the story. Circle the letter in front of the correct answer.

1. Mack and Ian each write about _____.
   a. completely different things that happened
   b. the thing that their dad said that day
   c. the same things that happened that day
   d. how delicious the bass tasted

2. When Ian swims to shore, Mack thinks _____.
   a. it is a wise thing to do
   b. Ian is confused and going the wrong way
   c. he should jump out of the canoe
   d. the water looks refreshing

3. Ian thinks that the cry of the loon is _____.
   a. weird
   b. disturbing
   c. wonderful
   d. frightening

4. Because bears try to get their food, the boys and their father _____.
   a. sleep inside the tent
   b. swim out into the lake
   c. are unable to sleep
   d. keep a big fire going

5. If their father suggests going wilderness camping again next year, Mack will probably _____.
   a. be the first one packed to go
   b. take along a bird book
   c. find something else he has to do
   d. ask Ian not to complain so much

Natural Tricks

Sometimes your eyes can play tricks on you. Other times, what you are seeing may be playing tricks on your eyes! This is the case with many plants and animals that use disguises and tricks. They do this to avoid their enemies, find food, and mate.

Some animals that are not dangerous can mimic animals that are poisonous to avoid predators. Other animals that *are* dangerous can mimic harmless animals or plants. Some moths look like hornets so that birds will leave them alone. One even has a fake stinger! One insect can make its hind end appear to be its head. When it jumps, it goes in the opposite direction from the one its predator anticipates. A certain spider will create fake, or decoy, spiders in its web to ward off danger. It builds the decoy spiders with masses of silk and pieces of dead insects. Predators will often attack the fake spiders instead of the real one.

So the next time you see a stick get up and walk away, a leaf that catches an insect for a meal, or a pair of eyes that turn out to be a pair of wings, you will know you've been deceived by nature!

Go on to next page.

Directions

Rewrite each sentence. Use a word with the same meaning from the Word List in place of the underlined words.

Word List
ward   disguises   mimic   predators

1. Many animals use <u>methods to hide their true identity</u> to trick prey.

_____

2. Others use trickery to protect themselves from <u>those that would eat them</u>.

_____

3. Some harmless animals will <u>pretend to be</u> poisonous ones, while dangerous animals will do the opposite.

_____

4. Animals use these tricks not only to <u>turn aside, or scare</u> off attackers, but also to find food and to mate.

_____

_____

Choose the word that best fits each sentence. Write the word in the blank.

5. Some animals are protected because they are _____.

   harmless   poisonous   predators

6. Animals can become prey because they are _____ by a trick.

   deceived   delivered   denied

7. One insect jumps in the opposite direction from the one its attacker _____.

   admits   allows   anticipates

8. The spider's _____ trick is an amazing example of animal trickery.

   web   decoy   spinning

Greener Grass

Patty was very excited about staying overnight at Veronica's home. Veronica lived across from a park in a big apartment. She had her own bathroom and telephone.

"It must be wonderful to be Veronica," Patty thought as she and her sister, Margie, cleaned their room. Then she packed the overnight bag her mother was letting her use. She would have to tell Veronica that it was hers. She hated lying to her new friend, but she couldn't admit she had no luggage. It was bad enough sharing a room in a house with one bathroom.

When the chauffeur carried the bag to the long black car, Patty felt glamorous as she looked back at Margie's open mouth and Mother's suspicious face.

A maid in a crisp black uniform met Patty at the door and took her to Veronica's room. Soon the maid called them to lunch at a table set just for them. Then the chauffeur drove them to a stable, where an instructor gave them riding lessons. Patty met Veronica's parents late that afternoon as they left the apartment for the evening.

That night Veronica asked Patty many questions. "You actually have a little sister?" Veronica said.

"Yes," Patty admitted. "And I have to eat every meal at the table with her and my parents."

"It sounds very nice," Veronica said. "May I visit you sometime? It sounds like a very nice life."

Go on to next page.

Directions

Answer each question about the story. Circle the letter in front of the correct answer.

1. Compared to Patty's home, Veronica's home is _____.
   a. not nearly as fancy
   b. a house, not just an apartment
   c. farther from the park
   d. much more expensive

2. Patty is afraid Veronica will think that she is _____.
   a. poor
   b. a snob
   c. lazy
   d. unfriendly

3. Patty thinks that Veronica's life is very _____.
   a. lonely
   b. difficult
   c. glamorous
   d. boring

4. At Veronica's house, the girls are almost always with _____.
   a. Margie
   b. the servants
   c. Veronica's parents
   d. Patty's mother

5. Veronica says that Patty's life sounds nice because Veronica is _____.
   a. eager to avoid people
   b. a very lonely girl
   c. always lying to Patty
   d. waited on hand and foot

It's an Illusion!

Have you ever put a pencil in a glass of water? If you did, did the pencil look bent? The pencil wasn't actually bent, but it appeared that way. This is an optical illusion, or an illusion sensed with your eyes.

You can make your own optical illusion with a piece of white cardboard, some string, and markers. Cut a circle from the cardboard about three to four inches in diameter. Draw a picture of a bird on one side of the circle. Now draw a cage large enough to hold the bird on the other side of the circle. Draw the cage upside down from the way you drew the bird. Punch one hole at each side of the cardboard, and attach a piece of string about eight inches long to each side by tying it through the hole. Be sure your drawing is right side up and that the strings are at opposite sides of the disc. First, twirl the strings, and then pull gently on both strings at the same time. The disc will spin, and the bird will appear in the cage.

There are other neat tricks you can play on your eyes. Flip books have the same picture on each page, but with a small change, so that when you flip the pages, the pictures appear to be moving. Your school or local library will have books that can show you many other fun ideas.

Go on to next page.

Name_____   Date_____

Directions

Read each sentence. Choose a word from the Word List that has the same meaning as the word or words in bold print. Write the word on the line.

Word List
optical   illusion   disc   diameter

1. The tricks discussed in this story are **of or have to do with sight**.

   _____

2. You can create your own **trick that fools one of the senses**.

   _____

3. The **distance across** for your circle should be three to
   four inches.

   _____

4. When you spin the **circular shape**, it will show you an illusion.

   _____

Write *true* or *false* next to each sentence.

5. _____ An illusion is something that is not real.

6. _____ An optical illusion is one that fools all the senses.

7. _____ To make the trick in the story, you should draw the bird

   inside the cage.

8. _____ There are many kinds of optical illusions.

9. _____ The eyes are the only sense that can be fooled.

10. _____ When you put a pencil in a glass of water, the pencil will bend.

Wait and See

Have you ever been worried about something that you *think* is going to happen? Then, when the time came, perhaps what you thought would happen did not happen. It may be that what really did happen was a good thing.

Many times people find themselves getting very emotional about things that have not even happened yet. These are things that may or may not happen. When people think they know what is going to happen, they can waste a lot of time fretting  about nothing. Most of the time, this kind of worry is caused by new experiences. Maybe you think that you won't know what to do in a new situation. You may believe that everyone else will know just what to do while you will be the only one who is unsure. It is true that some people don't worry about anything. They embrace new ideas and experiences without fear. However, it is good to remember that most people feel the same way that you do.

You might try to think of what the worst possible situation could be. Prepare yourself for it. Keep in mind, however, that the worst-case scenario is not very likely. The real outcome may be good or bad. There is nothing you can do about it anyway, so you might as well go into it with an open mind. Be an optimist! Look for good things in new experiences, and you will probably find them. Remember that if the experience is not a good one, you'll know not to do it again. Still, you will have had the experience. If you talk yourself out of a new experience before it happens, well, you will never know!

Go on to next page.

Name _____   Date _____

Directions

Read each clue. Choose a word from the Word List that fits each clue. Write the words in the puzzle.

Word List

emotional   fretting   unsure   embrace
scenario   outcome   optimist   situation

ACROSS:
2. a possible scene
4. the way things are
6. uncertain
7. with feeling
8. to take up willingly

DOWN:
1. worrying
3. one who hopes for the best
5. result

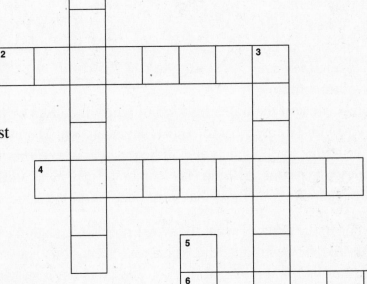

Camp Lakota

In the Weeds

When Sandy saw how difficult it was for Miss Mapleton to weed her flower garden, she stopped and volunteered to help. She worked in the garden a good part of one Saturday, but when it got too dim that evening to see what she was doing, they had cleared the weeds from only a small portion. Miss Mapleton would work beside Sandy a while, but then she would have to stop and rest. She was clearly not used to physical labor.

"I must pay you for all this fine help," Miss Mapleton would say. Then Sandy would pretend that pulling weeds was more fun than anything else she could do with her Saturday, and she refused to take a thing.

"Then you must come to dinner soon," Miss Mapleton would say. That conversation made Sandy want to avoid helping again, but every time she saw the woman out struggling against the weeds, Sandy would go and help. Each time she had to refuse money and a meal.

"I don't know why you won't at least take a meal as a reward for your good deed," Sandy's friend Trudy would say. Finally, Sandy explained very softly.

"You must never tell anyone. I ate Miss Mapleton's cooking once. I'm not looking for any reward, but I don't think I should be punished, either."

Go on to next page.

Directions

Answer each question about the story. Circle the letter in front of the correct answer.

1. Sandy begins helping Miss Mapleton because she _____.
   a. feels sorry for her
   b. wants a reward from Miss Mapleton
   c. loves pulling weeds from flower gardens
   d. is very hungry and wants a meal

2. After the first Saturday's weeding, Miss Mapleton's garden is _____.
   a. completely free of weeds
   b. nearly ruined
   c. full of good things to eat
   d. still in need of much weeding

3. Before she offers Sandy a meal, Miss Mapleton wants to _____.
   a. help weed Sandy's garden
   b. ask Trudy to help, too
   c. keep working all night
   d. pay Sandy for working

4. Sandy doesn't want Trudy to _____.
   a. help in Miss Mapleton's garden
   b. tell what Sandy said about Miss Mapleton's cooking
   c. tell their friends that Sandy was helping Miss Mapleton
   d. pretend that weeding is fun

5. Sandy thinks that the meals Miss Mapleton cooks are _____.
   a. very delicious
   b. more than Sandy deserves
   c. not good to eat
   d. a good reward

Helping Habits

Lending a helping hand is always a good idea. You don't have to wait for someone to ask for help to offer yours. Every day there are ways for you to help your parents, your friends, and others in your life.

The benefits of helping another person in need are more than first meet the eye. Of course, we all know it's the nice thing to do. Think about yourself in a situation where you might need help. Then imagine how you would feel if someone helped you. At the same time, helping other people helps you in ways you may not have considered. When you reach out to other people, you always feel better about yourself. It gives your life more meaning and brings you out of your own small world. You may think of a way to surprise someone with unexpected help. Planning to help someone can give you something to look forward to. Helping other people is a great way to make friends, too. Even a seemingly small thing, like helping someone to pick up dropped books or groceries, will bring a smile of appreciation from the recipient. The next time you see that person, you can bet he or she will remember your courtesy, and it will bring another smile—to both of you.

You can help others out of a small predicament or a great calamity. You can help by making sure you pull your own weight or by helping to lighten someone else's load as well. The choice is always yours. People remember those who are there with a helping hand, and someday when you need help, they will return the favor.

Go on to next page.

Directions

Think about the passage you read. Then fill in the blanks of the following paragraph with words from the Word List.

Word List

seemingly   benefits   calamity   appreciation
situation   recipient   courtesy   predicament

Helping someone else out of a difficult **1)** _____ is a nice thing

to do. Even the **2)** _____ small things that you do for others can

bring you many **3)** _____. Sometimes you may help someone out

of a small **4)** _____. Other times, you may find yourself helping

someone with a great **5)** _____. In either case, you can be sure the

6) _____ of your help will be grateful for your **7)** _____.

That person's **8)** _____ will be your reward.

Use the Word List above to choose the correct word for each meaning. Write your choice on the line.

9. one who receives_____

10. kindness_____

11. with an appearance that may or may not be real _____

12. extreme misfortune; disaster_____

13. things that are of help _____

14. a set of circumstances _____

15. a feeling or expression of gratitude _____

16. a difficult situation _____

Lucky Puppy

On his way to school, Michael saw Ben Shaw's new puppy running from Mrs. Smithers' old cat. He stopped to see that the puppy would be okay. He smiled when Max, the cat, stopped at the sidewalk and yawned at the puppy fleeing up the street.

On his way home from school, Michael saw the puppy again, but this time it was way over on a street near a park. "This is too far from home for Ben's new puppy to be playing," Michael thought. "The dog must still think it is running from Max and is lost."

Just then, the puppy ran out in the street and almost got hit by a car. Michael waited until the light changed and then crossed to find the puppy. It had fallen into a cement well built around a basement window in a big building. People were walking right past the window well and couldn't hear the puppy yipping over the traffic from the street. Michael found it because he was looking for it. Carefully he lifted it out and carried it home in his arms.

Michael met Ben and Mrs. Smithers about a block from their neighborhood. "Oh!" Mrs. Smithers cried. "You found the puppy. We've been looking all over."

When Michael explained what happened, Ben called him a hero. So did Mrs. Smithers. Michael didn't feel like a hero. "What would you have done?" he asked. "Anyone would have helped the puppy."

Go on to next page.

Name _____   Date _____

Directions

Answer each question about the story. Circle the letter in front of the correct answer.

1. Michael is not worried about the puppy in the morning because _____.
   a. it is much bigger than the cat
   b. the cat is too slow to catch it
   c. it runs into Ben's house
   d. the cat stops chasing it

2. No one else hears the puppy in the window well because it _____.
   a. has fallen asleep in there
   b. cannot be heard over the traffic
   c. jumps out and runs somewhere else
   d. is trying to hide from everyone

3. Michael thinks that when he sees the puppy over near the park, it _____.
   a. thinks the cat is still after it
   b. is on its way home
   c. has been hit by a car
   d. had followed Michael to school earlier

4. Ben and Mrs. Smithers think that Michael is a hero because he _____.
   a. saves them the trouble of finding the puppy
   b. laughs at Mrs. Smithers' cat
   c. waits for the traffic light to change
   d. rescues Ben's puppy before it is hurt

5. Michael thinks that heroes do things that _____.
   a. anyone would do
   b. don't really help anyone
   c. other people wouldn't do
   d. help people, not dogs

Taking a Load Off

Carmen's mother walked in the door and collapsed on the sofa, rubbed her fingers across her forehead, and sat still for a moment. Soon, she got up and went into the kitchen to begin dinner preparations. "Carmen," she called. "Would you please come out here and empty the dishwasher?"

"Oh, Mom!" moaned Carmen. "I always have to empty the dishwasher. Why do I have to do everything?"

Her mother put her head around the corner and glared at Carmen. "*You* do everything? I want you to think about that one."

Carmen got up and began unloading the dishwasher and putting the dishes in the cupboards. What was her mother angry about? Carmen did unload the dishwasher a lot—not always, but a lot. She looked at her mother out of the corner of her eye. She did look tired; she was rubbing her back and she moved slowly. She must have had a difficult day; she was on her feet most of the time at the store. Suddenly Carmen thought of a way that she could help her mother to feel better, and she waited for the next day with anticipation.

When Carmen got home from school the next afternoon, she straightened the house and got some things from the cupboard for a simple dinner. She went to her mother's room and found her slippers, heated some water for tea, and put a tea bag in a cup. When her mother walked in the door, Carmen took her purse and instructed her to sit down on the sofa. Then Carmen removed her mother's shoes and put her fluffy slippers on her sore feet. Finally, she brought her speechless mother a cup of piping hot tea.

"I already started dinner," said Carmen, "so you can rest for a while."

"Well, Carmen!" exclaimed her mother. "This is the most wonderful surprise I could ever have! Thank you so much!"

Carmen just smiled. It made her feel good to know that she had been the cause of her mother's happiness—and it had not been difficult at all!

Go on to next page.

Directions

Answer each question about the story. Circle the letter in front of the correct answer.

1. What did Carmen realize while she was unloading the dishwasher?
   a. that she really did do all the work
   b. that her mother was not a good worker
   c. that she could do more to help her mother
   d. that her mother did not like her job

2. What is *anticipation*?
   a. dread
   b. looking forward
   c. concern
   d. caution

3. Because helping her mother made her feel good, Carmen will probably _____.
   a. try to do it more often
   b. not do it again
   c. ask for something in return
   d. do it for everyone she knows

Write *true* or *false* next to each sentence.

4. _____ Carmen does all the housework.

5. _____ Carmen never does any housework.

6. _____ Carmen's mother is on her feet most of the day.

7. _____ Carmen is not sure how she feels at the end of the story.

8. _____ Both Carmen and her mother are happy at the end of the story.

The Three Experts

Once upon a time, there were three men who all lived in the same village by the sea. Each of the men was an expert at one thing, but each had begun to believe that he was an expert at all things. Since they lived on the ocean, it was a good thing to be an expert sailor. Though these three men were not great sailors, they challenged each other to sail around the reef that encircled their village. Now, it happened that it was winter and a storm was brewing in which even the real experts would not sail. They advised the three men to wait until spring, but the men were too proud and stubborn, and so they set sail anyway.

As predicted, the storm was too much for these inexperienced sailors, and they all found themselves washed ashore on the same island. The men were cold and hungry, and each set out alone to do what he was expert at doing. One went hunting and caught enough meat for all of the men. Another built a strong shelter large enough for a family. The last man managed to find wood and start a roaring fire without even a flint. The man with the meat could not eat it, for he had no fire. The man with the shelter was hungry and still cold, though protected from the wind. The man with the fire was warm, but very hungry.

As night came on, the man by the fire fell asleep. He was awakened by the sound of voices. The hunter had crept to the fire to cook some of his food. The man in the shelter had smelled the meat cooking and had come to demand some.

"It seems to me," said the man with the fire, "that we are all so proud that we might die out here. Perhaps our shipwrecks should have taught us all some humility."

So the three men moved the fire and the meat to the shelter and were able to survive until the spring, when they were rescued by those who really did know how to sail.

Go on to next page.

Directions

Answer each question about the story. Circle the letter in front of the correct answer.

1. Why was it a bad time for the men to sail?
   a. There were no boats.
   b. The water was too low.
   c. It was winter.
   d. There were no sailors.

2. What happened when the men went sailing?
   a. One of the men won the contest.
   b. Two of the men got home, but one was lost.
   c. The men became expert sailors.
   d. All three men were washed up on an island.

3. Which of these describes the three men's expertise?
   a. hunting, building, and making fire
   b. hunting, sailing, and making fire
   c. building, making a fire, and cooking
   d. sailing, cooking, and making a fire

4. What is *humility*?
   a. being embarrassed
   b. being humble
   c. being hungry
   d. being proud

5. The men would not have survived without _____.
   a. fighting
   b. sailing
   c. cooperating
   d. talking

Helping Children

Years ago, children without parents were taken in by neighbors and raised as part of the family. These orphaned children could usually find good homes and have happy lives even if they were never actually adopted by their new family. As time went on, many people moved off farms and into cities, like New York, to work. Neighbors did not know each other as well as they once had. People were paid low wages, and prices for food and lodging were very high. This was not a good time for most people, but it was a worse time for the children. Many of them ended up on the streets at the age of five or six. Some went to work in factories. Some shined shoes. Others sold matches or newspapers. Life was harsh for these children.

A man named Charles Brace started the Children's Aid Society in New York. He had heard of trains that took children to the country and "out West" to new homes. He had a plan to send hundreds of these orphans on orphan trains to the West. At this time, in 1853, the West only went as far as what today we call the Midwest. Children were given new clothes and loaded onto the trains in groups. These groups went from town to town, where the local people could gather and look the children over. People who wanted a child could choose one. These prospective parents were supposed to meet certain criteria to show that they would be good parents, but many times, their willingness to take in an orphan was enough. Some children were taken into loving homes. Others were taken for servants and abused. Most found a better life than they had had in the city.

For some children, the experience of going on the orphan trains was frightening and humiliating. Often, they had no idea what was happening to them. Many times, when there were two or more children from the same family, they were separated. Some placements worked better than others did. Several children had to be moved many times before they found a good home. Overall, however, for seventy-six years, the orphan trains were successful in giving good homes to thousands of New York's children.

Go on to next page.

Directions

Read each clue. Choose a word from the Word List that fits each clue.
Write the words in the puzzle.

Word List
humiliating   orphaned   abused   criteria
prospective   placements   wages   willingness

ACROSS:
1. without parents
7. being ready to act gladly
8. rules by which something can be judged

DOWN:
2. likely to become
3. causing hurt to one's pride
4. mistreated
5. payment for work
6. arrangements

The Wand

People were running everywhere in the streets in every direction. Women carried and dragged their little children. Buildings fell all around as the earth shook violently. No one knew where to go, but everyone wanted to get away from the danger.

On a corner, there was an elderly man with his hand caught under some fallen rock. "Help me!" he cried over and over again to everyone who passed. Most people didn't even see him as they rushed by with their own concerns. Some people did see the man, but they couldn't spare the time to help him; they wanted to save themselves.

A young man with his wife and three children approached. The children were crying, and the man and his wife were desperately trying to keep them moving quickly. Then one of the children saw the old man and stopped to see why he was not running.

"Please, little girl," the old man begged. "Get your parents to move these rocks so that I can move my arm."

The little girl tugged repeatedly on her father's shirt and insisted that he stop, until finally, the father turned around and saw the helpless old man. He ran to him and struggled with the rocks until he had removed them from the man's hand. To the younger man's amazement, he saw something like a wand in the old man's hand. The old man weakly raised the arm with the wand, and the earthquake ceased immediately.

In the incredible stunned silence that followed, everyone could hear the old man when he said, "Thank you, my son. As you can see, you have saved far more than the life of one old man."

Go on to next page.

Directions

Answer each question about the story. Circle the letter in front of the correct answer.

1. What is happening in the story?
   a. A volcano has erupted.
   b. There is an earthquake.
   c. A meteor has struck Earth.
   d. A tidal wave is coming.

2. Why are the people running in every direction?
   a. They can't see anything.
   b. Someone is telling them to.
   c. They don't know where to go.
   d. The shaking is moving them.

3. Why isn't the old man running?
   a. His legs are broken.
   b. His legs are caught under rocks.
   c. He is too tired to run.
   d. His arm is caught under rocks.

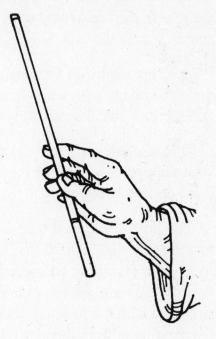

4. What does the old man have in his hand?
   a. a wand
   b. a cane
   c. a ring
   d. a note

5. What might the people who did not stop for the old man be thinking at the end of the story?
   a. that they are glad they did not stop
   b. that they are afraid of the old man
   c. that he could have stopped the earthquake much sooner
   d. that the young man should not have stopped

Dreamland

Caroline came to a very strange woods, indeed. The trees had big blue and purple leaves shaped like half-moons, circles, squares, and stars! They moved slowly back and forth like fans. The trunks of the trees had big, dark jewels set in rough silver bark. Through the trees, the sky looked like green water, and it gurgled as the leaves stirred in the air.

All at once, the ground beside her burst open, filling the air with pink snow. Up out of the ground came a huge, fat caterpillar with zebra stripes and an orange head like a smiling cookie.

"Oh my, oh my!" Caroline cried. "Do you live in this lovely place?"

The cookie head stopped smiling. "Do not!" it said. "I certainly do not! What's lovely about blue trees and a green sky? I used to live here! Used to! Until you and your silly dream did this to the place. Please wake up so this place can be normal again."

So Caroline did wake up, and there on her pillow was a big, blue, star-shaped leaf!

Directions

Answer each question about the story. Circle the letter in front of the correct answer.

1. The colors of the leaves on the trees are _____.
   a. green and pink
   b. blue and purple
   c. orange and silver
   d. black and white

2. The sky gurgles because _____.
   a. the caterpillar is drinking it
   b. the snow makes it too cold
   c. it is laughing at Caroline
   d. the leaves are stirring around

3. The caterpillar comes _____.
   a. up out of the ground
   b. swimming out of the sky
   c. down from the trees
   d. out of a fat, star-shaped leaf

4. The caterpillar says that the woods are strange because _____.
   a. it has come to live there
   b. the pink ground grows odd things
   c. Caroline's dream has changed it
   d. the ground has burst open

5. When Caroline awakens she finds _____.
   a. a star-shaped leaf on her pillow
   b. herself in a normal woods
   c. a caterpillar in her hand
   d. a smiling cookie in her room

Phantom Frights

One of the great mysteries of the sea is the existence of phantom ships. These unoccupied ships seem to drift the ocean as if piloted by ghosts. The ships have been seen all over the world in every kind of weather and by all kinds of people. One thing they all seem to have in common is their ability to send shivers up the spines of those who witness them.

One explanation is that they are simply ships that have been abandoned by their crews. In the mist of the ocean or in a storm, they certainly must be eerie sights. The U.S. Coast Guard in the 1930s destroyed many of these ships in order to make waterways safer. After this, sightings of phantom ships declined. However, this does not explain the sightings that continue.

Many of the reports of phantom ships are of ships that no longer exist. These ships have been destroyed by fire or shipwreck. There is a story of one vessel whose owner was engaged in some illegal activity. Upon finding himself surrounded by warships, the skipper blew up the ship and himself. Still, this ship has often been sighted, drifting the water in flames.

Why would so many report seeing ships if they are not there? Perhaps it is just one of those hazards of tired eyes on watch. Maybe after looking out over the endless blue for hours, the eyes begin to play tricks. Even so, whole crews have reported many of these sightings. Now, how does one explain that?

Go on to next page.

Directions

Think about the passage you read. Then fill in the blanks of the following paragraph with words from the Word List.

Word List
abandoned   unoccupied   waterways   phantom
declined   illegal   skipper   existence

The **1)** _____ of ghostly ships on the sea remains a mystery.

They may simply be **2)** _____ ships. Most of these were destroyed

by the Coast Guard in order to clean up the **3)** _____. Sightings of

4) _____ ships **5)** _____ after the Coast Guard was

through. Some sightings continue, however. One vessel whose **6)** _____

was involved in some **7)** _____ activity was blown up. This ship is

still seen, **8)** _____ and in flames, riding the waves of the ocean.

Write *fact* or *opinion* in front of each sentence about the passage.

9. _____ These unoccupied ships seem to drift the ocean as if

    piloted by ghosts.

10. _____ The ships have been destroyed by fire or shipwreck.

11. _____ The skipper blew up the ship and himself.

12. _____ Even so, whole crews have reported many of these sightings.

13. _____ In the mist of the ocean or in a storm, they certainly must

    be eerie sights.

Twin Tricks

"What's your name?" Peter asked the new boy who moved in next door.

The boy pushed his blond hair to the left of his forehead with his right hand. "I'm Todd," he said. "Want to play some basketball?"

"I can't," Peter said. "I have to go to Dr. Donaldson's. Boy, I dread going to the dentist."

"Hey," Todd said, "that's our new dentist. I'm going there today myself. I look forward to it. My teeth feel so clean after going to the dentist."

"Let's get to Dr. Donaldson's!" Peter's dad called.

As Peter walked into the waiting room, he couldn't believe whom he saw walking out of the inner office. "It's Todd!" he thought. "Have you already seen the dentist?" Peter cried.

"Yeah," the blond boy said, using his left hand to brush his hair to the right. "I'm glad that's over!"

"How did you do that, Todd? You were standing in your front yard when we left a few minutes ago."

The boy looked surprised himself. Then he smiled broadly. "It's a special power I have," he said. "I rub my right elbow, and bingo! I travel."

When Peter came out of Dr. Donaldson's inner office, Todd was sitting there beside a boy who looked just like him. "I hear you met my brother, Terry, and that he's up to our old twin tricks."

Go on to next page.

Directions

Answer each question about the story. Circle the letter in front of the correct answer.

1. What is Terry's special power?
   a. He really can rub his elbows and move to another place.
   b. He can get in ahead of people at the dentist.
   c. He is an old friend of Dr. Donaldson.
   d. He has a brother who looks almost exactly like him.

2. How can you tell that Peter went right to the dentist after leaving Todd?
   a. He got there after Todd did.
   b. Todd said that he was going there that day.
   c. Peter's dad said it was time to go there.
   d. Todd had never been to see Dr. Donaldson before.

3. Which of these is a clue that Peter misses?
   a. The twins brush their hair in different directions.
   b. Todd likes to play basketball.
   c. Both twins have blond hair.
   d. Todd says he is going to see Dr. Donaldson that same day.

4. Which is another clue that Peter misses?
   a. Each twin has a name that begins with *T*.
   b. Todd lives right next door.
   c. Todd is right-handed; Terry is left-handed.
   d. Todd hadn't told Peter about Terry.

5. What is still another clue that Peter misses?
   a. Todd is new to the neighborhood.
   b. Todd likes going to the dentist; Terry does not.
   c. Dr. Donaldson's office is only minutes away.
   d. Todd has blond hair, and so does Terry.

Clubhouse Mystery

"Hey, Josh, where are the comics I left here yesterday?" asked Ben.

"I don't know. I'm looking for the soda. I was sure there were at least five cans here last time I checked," answered Josh. "Something funny is going on here. Where's all our stuff going?"

Josh and Ben continued to notice certain items missing from the clubhouse over the next week. They asked Curtis and Dwayne if they knew anything about it, but both boys said they hadn't even been at the house that week.

Then one day as Josh came home from school, he happened to glance into the backyard and noticed that his younger brother, Billy, had set up a little shelter from pieces of wood and tar paper left over from their father's latest building project. Josh went over for a close inspection, laughing to himself at Billy's ingenuity. Josh was impressed by how well Billy had constructed his fort. As he looked inside, however, Josh stopped laughing and flushed with anger. He saw the comics, the soda, and a few other items that had turned up missing from his own clubhouse.

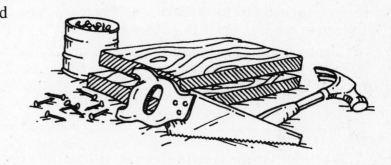

Later, Josh confronted Billy with the evidence. "So what's the idea, Billy?" asked Josh. "You know that stuff isn't yours. You're not even allowed into our clubhouse."

"I know," said Billy, his lip trembling. "But you never let me in your clubhouse, so I had to make my own. I didn't have any of the cool stuff you had, and you had so much, so I took some. I know it was wrong, Josh. I'm sorry."

Josh felt a sudden swell of affection for his little brother. "Hey, don't worry about it, kid. You did a great job on your fort. If you promise not to take any more of our stuff, I'll help you get what you need in the future. Deal?"

"Deal," said Billy, smiling from ear to ear.

Go on to next page.

Directions

Read each sentence. Choose a word from the Word List that has the same meaning as the word or words in bold print. Write the word on the line.

Word List
flushed   evidence   ingenuity   inspection
affection   constructed   confronted   impressed

1. Billy's building **had a strong, favorable effect on** his brother, Josh._____

2. Josh thought Billy had used a lot of **cleverness** in his building. _____

3. Josh went over to Billy's fort for a closer **look**. _____

4. The fort was **built** with leftover wood and tar paper. _____

5. Josh **turned red in the face** with anger when he saw what Billy had taken.

_____

6. Josh had all the **facts** he needed to know that Billy had been in the clubhouse.

_____

7. When Josh **came face-to-face** with Billy, Billy began to cry. _____

8. Josh felt a swell of **love** for his younger brother, and was not angry anymore.

_____

Write *true* or *false* next to each sentence.

9. _____ Josh and Billy were brothers.

10. _____ Josh thought Billy had done a good job on his fort.

11. _____ Josh helped Billy build his fort.

12. _____ Ben discovered the missing items in Billy's fort.

13. _____ Josh and Billy made an agreement.

Mystery Tree

The party ended with a treasure hunt. Mrs. Mallone had hidden two movie tickets. The two members of the team that found them first got to use them. All three teams were handed the first clue to read together. It said,

"They're really not too hard to see
if you don't bark under the wrong tree."

Everyone ran outside and began racing from tree to tree. Ricardo was the first to spot three envelopes stuck in the bark of one tree. He and Cathy read the clue inside the one with their names on it. It said,

"You should look under—if you're really trying—
another tree that should be crying."

When Sharon found the same clue and read it to Bill, she cried, "The big apple tree by the back door always drips rain on people when they come out!" They were the first to find the last clue in one of the envelopes under the apple tree. It said,

"The first clue could have led you to the prize!
This analogy may help open your eyes:
Sour apples are to sweet figs as *outside* is to _____."

When Jackie and Tim got the clue, Tim yelled, "Follow me!" and ran in the house to a tall, tree-like plant by a window. Under it was one envelope. The two tickets were inside. "It's called a Weeping Fig tree," Tim explained.

Go on to next page.

www.svschoolsupply.com
© Steck-Vaughn Company
89
Unit VI: Mystery and Adventure
Improving Reading Comprehension 5, SV 5803-5

Directions

Answer each question about the story. Circle the letter in front of the correct answer.

1. Who are first to read the clue?
   a. Mr. and Mrs. Mallone
   b. Sharon and Bill
   c. all of the children
   d. Ricardo and Cathy

2. Why does everyone run outdoors after reading the first clue?
   a. It says to go outside.
   b. It suggests looking under a tree.
   c. It says to find a barking dog.
   d. They all need a second clue.

3. Why does the second clue lead Sharon to the apple tree?
   a. It says the tree might be crying.
   b. It says people could eat off the tree.
   c. The back door is mentioned.
   d. It begins to rain.

4. Which word is missing in the analogy?
   a. peel
   b. inside
   c. delicious
   d. outdoors

5. Which clues might lead to the place the tickets are found?
   a. only the first clue
   b. only the second clue
   c. only the third clue
   d. all of the clues

The Dream

The hideous monster stood only a few feet away from Braxton's hiding place. He knew he would have to step out and fight it, but he trembled with fear at the thought of fighting the mighty beast. Then, without further thought, he leapt out and brandished his sword. The monster roared and swiped at Braxton with its huge claws. Braxton managed to avoid the claws and duck in close to the monster. He eluded another swipe of the monster's mighty claws, and then fatally wounded it. He jumped out of the way just in time as the monster fell to the ground with a great thud.

Now Braxton had to get out of the cave he had come into to slay the monster. He wasn't sure which was the correct path to take, but after many attempts, he found himself at the opening of the cave. He was not out of danger yet, however. Huge bird-like creatures began to swoop down upon him, one by one. Luckily, he still had his sword, and he could fend them off, but how long could he last? All of a sudden, one of the creatures came at him from behind. He could feel himself being lifted from the ground, higher and higher, and then just as suddenly, he was dropped. He found himself falling fast toward the rocky ground.

Braxton rolled over in his sleep. The book he had been reading, *Monster Myths and Tales of Adventure*, was knocked to the floor, and Braxton woke with a start. "Whew!" he exclaimed. "I guess I'd better read something more tame before I go to sleep!" Then he went back to sleep.

Go on to next page.

Name _____   Date _____

Directions

Read each clue. Choose a word from the Word List to find an answer to fit each clue. Write the words in the puzzle.

Word List

hideous myths avoid fatally
slay leapt brandished fend

ACROSS:
2. stay away from
3. held out; waved
5. hold off; resist
6. kill
8. stories

DOWN:
1. to death
4. horrible; ugly
7. jumped

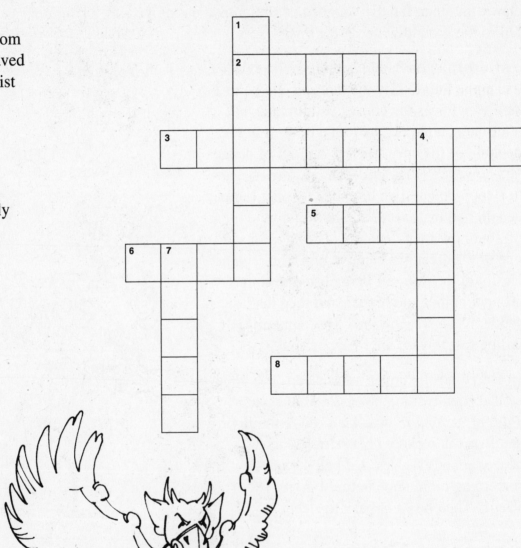

Ocean Adventure

When Emily and Rochelle got to the beach, Emily just could not stop exclaiming about how big the ocean was, or how blue. She was amazed at the softness of the sand. Every sea creature they found when they took a walk along the shore was of great interest to her. Emily was from Oklahoma and had never seen the ocean. She had studied it and seen pictures, but being there was something totally new!

During the week that Emily stayed with Rochelle, they visited the beach often. They collected shells, sand dollars, and beautifully colored rocks. They saw jellyfish, mussels, clams, starfish, and crabs on the beach at low tide. They even went on a boat trip. While on the water, they saw dozens of seals sunning themselves on the rocks and a huge whale in the distance. It seemed to Emily to be the most wonderful place in the world. She missed her family toward the end of the week, but she didn't know how she could leave the beautiful shore and all its treasures.

The day came when Emily had to go, however, so she and Rochelle said their good-byes. "I hope you can come back soon," said Rochelle.

"I hope so, too!" said Emily. "This has been an adventure I will never forget!"

Name _____   Date _____

Directions

Answer each question about the story. Circle the letter in front of the correct answer.

1. Where was Emily from?
   a. Utah
   b. Oklahoma
   c. California
   d. Maine

2. How long did Emily stay with Rochelle?
   a. a few weeks
   b. one week
   c. a few days
   d. a month

3. Why was Emily so amazed by the ocean?
   a. She had never seen it.
   b. She was amazed at everything.
   c. She had never seen such a large ocean.
   d. She had studied the ocean.

4. When Emily left, she was probably _____.
   a. tired of the ocean
   b. looking forward to visiting again
   c. tired of staying with Rochelle
   d. an expert on the ocean

5. Because of Emily's visit, Rochelle will most likely _____.
   a. appreciate more her life near the ocean
   b. stay away from the ocean for a while
   c. wish she did not live near the ocean
   d. invite the rest of her friends to visit

Improving Reading Comprehension
Grade 5
Answer Key

P. 7-8
1. brunt
2. pressured
3. challenged
4. unwilling
5. mischievous
6. b
7. c
8. d
9. remarks
10. realized
11. complained
Answers will vary. Students should use complete sentences and support their argument.

P. 9-10
1. benefits
2. situation
3. seemingly
4. appreciation
5. courtesy
6. benefits
7. situation
8. recipient
9. unexpected
10. appreciation
11. true
12. false
13. false
14. true
15. false
Answers will vary. Students should use complete sentences and address questions.

P. 12
1. b
2. d
3. a
4. b
5. c

P. 14
1. hostess
2. odyssey
3. misunderstood
4. lifelong
5. companion
6. mythological, or mythical
7. doubts
8. mythical, or mythological
9. lifelong
10. misunderstood
11. companion
12. doubts
13. mythological, or mythical
14. hostess
15. mythical, or mythological
16. odyssey

P. 16
1. c
2. b
3. a
4. d
5. c

P. 18
1. b
2. c
3. d
4. true
5. false
6. false
7. false
8. true

P. 20
1. d
2. b
3. a
4. d
5. a

P. 22
ACROSS
4. revolutionary
6. connection
8. issues
DOWN
1. participate
2. governor
3. dramatizing
5. senators
7. involved

P. 24
1. d
2. b
3. c
4. d
5. a

P. 26
1. d
2. a
3. b
4. c
5. a

P. 28
Sentences using the following words:
1. plotted
2. deceive
3. ledge
4. theory
Answers will vary.

P. 30
1. c
2. a
3. d
4. b
5. a

P. 32
1. severe
2. accomplishment
3. occupy
4. enjoyable
5. diary
6. document
7. true
8. false
9. true
10. false
11. false
12. false

P. 34
1. c
2. a
3. b
4. d
5. a

P. 36
ACROSS
5. humankind
6. envy
7. punishment
8. eternity
DOWN
1. anguish
2. plague
3. revenge
4. intrigue

P. 38
1. d
2. c
3. d
4. c
5. b

P. 40
1. d
2. b
3. c
4. d
5. c

P. 42
ACROSS
5. navigate
6. accomplished
7. uninterrupted
DOWN
1. fanfare
2. aviation
3. encountered
4. compensate
8. pursuit

P. 44
1. c
2. c
3. a
4. d
5. b

P. 46
Sentences using the following words:
1. perseverance
2. pursuing
3. achievement
4. goodwill
5. rookie
6. veteran
7. handicap
8. inspiring

P. 48
1. a
2. b
3. c
4. a
5. d

P. 50
1. celebrity
2. pressured
3. mischievous
4. unpopular
5. unwilling
6. taunt
7. brunt
8. surprisingly
9. fact
10. fact
11. opinion
12. opinion
13. fact

P. 52
1. c
2. a
3. b
4. c
5. d

P. 54
1. b
2. c
3. b
4. d
5. c

P. 56
1. regretted
2. midafternoon
3. disheartening
4. offhand
5. discussion
6. corresponded
7. false
8. true
9. true
10. true
11. false
12. true

P. 58
1. c
2. b
3. c
4. d
5. c

P. 60
Sentences using the
following words:
1. disguises
2. predators
3. mimic
4. ward
5. poisonous
6. deceived
7. anticipates
8. decoy

P. 62
1. d
2. a
3. c
4. b
5. b

P. 64
1. optical
2. illusion
3. diameter
4. disc
5. true
6. false
7. false
8. true
9. false
10. false

P. 66
ACROSS
2. scenario
4. situation
6. unsure
7. emotional
8. embrace
DOWN
1. fretting
3. optimist
5. outcome

P. 68
1. a
2. d
3. d
4. b
5. c

P. 70
1. situation
2. seemingly
3. benefits
4. predicament
5. calamity
6. recipient
7. courtesy
8. appreciation
9. recipient
10. courtesy
11. seemingly
12. calamity
13. benefits
14. situation
15. appreciation
16. predicament

P. 72
1. d
2. b
3. a
4. d
5. c

P. 74
1. c
2. b
3. a
4. false
5. false
6. true
7. false
8. true

P. 76
1. c
2. d
3. a
4. b
5. c

P. 78
ACROSS
1. orphaned
7. willingness
8. criteria
DOWN
2. prospective
3. humiliating
4. abused
5. wages
6. placements

P. 80
1. b
2. c
3. d
4. a
5. c

P. 82
1. b
2. d
3. a
4. c
5. a

P. 84
1. existence
2. abandoned
3. waterways
4. phantom
5. declined
6. skipper
7. illegal
8. unoccupied
9. opinion
10. fact
11. fact
12. fact
13. opinion

P. 86
1. d
2. c
3. a
4. c
5. b

P. 88
1. impressed
2. ingenuity
3. inspection
4. constructed
5. flushed
6. evidence
7. confronted
8. affection
9. true
10. true
11. false
12. false
13. true

P. 90
1. c
2. b
3. a
4. b
5. d

P. 92
ACROSS
2. avoid
3. brandished
5. fend
6. slay
8. myths
DOWN
1. fatally
4. hideous
7. leapt

P. 94
1. b
2. b
3. a
4. b
5. a